Culture War?

Culture War?

The Myth of a Polarized America

MORRIS P. FIORINA

STANFORD UNIVERSITY

WITH

SAMUEL J. ABRAMS

HARVARD UNIVERSITY

AND

JEREMY C. POPE

STANFORD UNIVERSITY

PEARSON
Longman

New York • Boston • San Francisco
London • Toronto • Sydney • Tokyo • Singapore • Madrid
Mexico City • Munich • Paris • Cape Town • Hong Kong • Montreal

Vice President and Publisher:	Priscilla McGeehon
Executive Editor:	Eric Stano
Acquisitions Editor:	Edward Costello
Senior Marketing Manager:	Elizabeth Fogarty
Managing Editor:	Bob Ginsberg
Production Manager:	Joseph Vella
Project Coordination, Text Design, and Electronic Page Makeup:	Thompson Steele Production Services, Inc.
Senior Cover Design Manager:	Nancy Danahy
Cover Design Manager:	John Callahan
Cover Designer:	Kay Petronio
Manufacturing Manager:	Mary Fischer
Printer and Binder:	Phoenix Color Corporation
Cover Printer:	Phoenix Color Corporation

Library of Congress Cataloging-in-Publication Data

ISBN 0-321-31773-4

On file at the Library of Congress

Please visit our website at http://www.ablongman.com.

ISBN 0-321-31773-4

1 2 3 4 5 6 7 8 9 10—PBT—07 06 05 04

To the tens of millions

of mainstream Americans

who have never heard

of the culture war

Contents

Preface

The late Senator Daniel Patrick Moynihan used to say that we all were entitled to our own opinions, but not to our own facts. This book uses simple facts to confront a distorted political debate in this country. Increasingly, we hear politicians, interest group leaders, and assorted "activists" speak half-truths to the American people. They tell us that the United States is split right down the middle, bitterly and deeply divided about national issues, when the truth is more nearly the opposite. Americans are closely divided, but we are not deeply divided, and we are closely divided because many of us are ambivalent and uncertain, and consequently reluctant to make firm commitments to parties, politicians, or policies. We divide evenly in elections or sit them out entirely because we instinctively seek the center while the parties and candidates hang out on the extremes.

How can the prevailing view assert the direct opposite? Mainly for want of contradiction by those who know better. We should not expect political actors to speak truthfully to us. For them, words are weapons, and the standard of success is electoral and legislative victory, not education or enlightenment. We may regret that perspective, but it should not surprise us. What is more surprising, and more disappointing, is that inaccurate claims and charges made by members of the political class go uncorrected by those who have some occupational responsibility to correct them, namely, members of the media and academic communities.

Increasingly, the media have abandoned their informational role in favor of an entertainment role. If colorful claims have news value, well then, why worry about their truth value? Don't let facts get in the way of a good story line. As for those of us in academia, we roll our eyes at the television, shake our heads while reading the newspapers, and lecture our students on the fallacies reported in the media, but few of us go beyond that. Mostly we talk to and write for each other.

In the past few years there have been increasing indications (see Chapter 1) that high-level political actors are beginning to believe in the distorted picture of American politics that they have helped to paint. This development threatens to make the distorted picture a self-fulfilling prophecy as a polarized political class abandons any effort to reach out toward the great middle of the country. That threat has motivated this ivory tower academic to attempt to provide his fellow citizens with a picture of American politics that is very different from the one they see portrayed on their televisions and described in their newspapers and magazines, a picture I think they will recognize as a more accurate reflection of their social surroundings.

My thanks to the Hoover Institution and Stanford University for the financial support that made this book possible. In particular, their support enabled me to engage two able, hard-working collaborators, Samuel Abrams and Jeremy Pope, who compiled and organized data, questioned my arguments and conclusions, and clarified the presentation. Thanks also to seminar participants at Harvard University, Northwestern University, and Stanford University for their helpful comments and suggestions about the analyses reported in these pages. Joshua Dunn, The College of William & Mary; Clyde Wilcox, Georgetown University; Jack Citrin, University of California, Berkley; Kent Jennings, University of California, Santa Barbara; and David Edwards, University of Texas reviewed the manuscript and provided useful comments. Sam Popkin offered valuable suggestions for making the argument clearer, and as always, Bonnie Honig urged me to give more thought to broader issues.

MORRIS P. FIORINA

A member of that tiny elite that comments publicly about political currents (probably some fraction of 1% of a population) spends most of his time in informal communication about politics with others in the same select group. He rarely encounters a conversation in which his assumptions of shared contextual grasp of political ideas are challenged. . . . It is largely from his informal communications that he learns how "public opinion" is changing and what the change signifies, and he generalizes facilely from these observations to the bulk of the broader public.

Philip Converse, "The Nature of Belief Systems in Mass Publics," in *Ideology and Discontent,* ed. David Apter (New York: Free Press, 1964): 206–261

Culture War?

CHAPTER 1

Culture War?

There is a religious war going on in this country, a cultural war as critical to the kind of nation we shall be as the Cold War itself, for this war is for the soul of America. *

With those ringing words insurgent candidate Pat Buchanan fired up his supporters at the 1992 Republican National Convention. To be sure, not all the assembled delegates cheered Buchanan's call to arms, which was at odds with the "kinder, gentler" image that incumbent President George H. W. Bush had attempted to project. Indeed, Republican professionals expressed concern about the "family values" emphasis of the convention in general, and Buchanan's remarks in particular.[1] Their concerns proved well

---

* This quotation appears in slightly different forms throughout the literature, probably because it was written up differently by journalists who covered the speech and/or read slightly different versions of it. This version is quoted in Nancy Davis and Robert Robinson, "A War for America's Soul?" In Rhys Williams, ed., *Cultural Wars in American Politics* (New York: Aldine de Gruyter, 1997); 39.
[1] Andrew Rosenthal, "The 1992 Campaign: Issues—'Family Values,'" *New York Times*, September 21, 1992: 1.

founded: elections analysts later included the Convention and Buchanan's fiery words among the factors contributing to the defeat of President Bush, albeit of lesser importance than the struggling economy and repudiation of his "Read my lips, no new taxes" pledge.[2]

In the years since Buchanan's declaration of cultural war the idea of a clash of cultures has become a common theme in discussions of American politics. Most commentators use the culture war metaphor to refer to a displacement or supercession of the classic economic conflicts that animated twentieth-century politics in the advanced democracies by newly emergent moral and religious ones. The literature generally attributes Buchanan's inspiration to a 1991 book, *Culture Wars*, by sociologist James Davison Hunter, who divided Americans into the culturally "orthodox" and the culturally "progressive" and argued that increasing conflict was inevitable.[3] In a later book provocatively titled *Before the Shooting Begins*, Hunter writes

> . . . *when cultural impulses this momentous vie against each other to dominate public life, tension, conflict, and perhaps even violence are inevitable.*[4]

Not surprisingly, no one has embraced the concept of the culture war more enthusiastically than the journalistic community, ever alert for subjects that have "news value." Conflict, of course,

---

2 Paul Abramson, John Aldrich, and David Rohde, *Change and Continuity in the 1992 Elections.* (Washington, DC: CQ Press, 1994): 43–44, 137. For a detailed analysis of the association between family values issues and the 1992 voting see Laura Arnold and Herbert Weisberg, "Parenthood, Family Values, and the 1992 Presidential Election." *American Politics Quarterly* 24 (1996): 194–220.

3 *Culture Wars: The Struggle to Define America* (New York: Basic Books, 1991).

4 *Before the Shooting Begins: Searching for Democracy in America's Culture War* (New York Free Press. 1995): xx.

is high in news value. Disagreement, division, polarization, battles, and war make good copy. Agreement, consensus, moderation, compromise, and peace do not. Thus, the concept of a culture war fits well with the news sense of journalists who cover American politics. Their reports tell us that contemporary voters are deeply divided on moral issues:

> . . . *the real emotional splits in the country lie in gut-level social issues: They are the topics that move Americans in their everyday lives, and the ones that actually draw the lines separating the two parties today.*[5]

> *The divide went deeper than politics. It reached into the nation's psyche. . . . It was the moral dimension that kept Bush in the race.*[6]

And close elections do not reflect indifferent, uncertain, or ambivalent voters; rather, close elections reflect evenly matched blocs of deeply committed partisans:

> *When George W. Bush took office, half the country cheered and the other half seethed.*[7]

> *Such political divisions cannot easily be shifted by any president, let alone in two years, because they reflect deep demographic divisions. . . . The 50-50 nation appears to be made*

---

[5] John Harwood and Shailagh Murray, "Split Society: Year After Year, The Big Divide In Politics Is Race," *Wall Street Journal*, December 19, 2002: A1.
[6] David Broder, "One Nation, Divisible; Despite Peace, Prosperity, Voters Agree to Disagree," *Washington Post*, November 8, 2000: A1.
[7] Jill Lawrence, "Behind Its United Front, Nation Divided As Ever," *USA Today*, February 18, 2002: A1.

up of two big, separate voting blocks, with only a small num-
ber of swing voters in the middle.[8]

The 2000 election brought us the familiar pictorial representation of the culture war in the form of the red and blue map of the
United States reproduced on the inside front cover of this book.
Vast areas of the southern and midwestern heartland emerged from
the election as Republican red. But the huge expanses of red terri-
tory contained relatively few people per square mile. The much
smaller areas of Democratic blue contained the more populous cos-
mopolitan states of the east and west coasts and the Great Lakes.
Commentators accompanied such colorful maps with polling fac-
toids intended to illustrate the cultural divide: the probability that
a white, gun-toting, born-again, rural southern male voted for Al
Gore was about as tiny as the probability that a feminist, agnostic,
professional, urban northern female voted for George W. Bush,
although few asked how many Americans fell into such narrowly
defined categories. For the most part pundits reified the different
colors on the map, treating them as *prima facie* evidence of deep
cultural divisions:

> *Bush knew that the landslide he had wished for in 2000 . . .*
> *had vanished into the values chasm separating the blue states*
> *from the red ones.*[9]

> *The Year of our Lord 2000 was the year of the map. . . . This*
> *election was Hollywood vs. Nashville, "Sex and the City" vs.*
> *"Touched by an Angel," National Public Radio vs. talk radio,*

---

[8] "On His High Horse," *Economist*, November 9, 2002: 25.
[9] John Kenneth White, *The Values Divide* (New Jersey: Chatham House, 2003): 171.

"Doonesbury" vs. "B.C.", "Hotel California" vs. "Okie From Muskogee." It was The New York Times vs. National Review Online, Dan Rather vs. Rush Limbaugh, Rosie O'Donnell vs. Dr. Laura, Barbra Streisand vs. Dr. James Dobson, the Supreme Court vs.—well, the Supreme Court.[10]

Tens of millions of good people in Middle America voted Republican. But if you look closely at that map you see a more complex picture. You see the state where James Byrd was lynch-dragged behind a pickup truck until his body came apart—it's red. You see the state where Matthew Shepard was crucified on a split-rail fence for the crime of being gay—it's red. You see the state where right-wing extremists blew up a federal office building and murdered scores of federal employ-ees—it's red. The state where an Army private who was thought to be gay was bludgeoned to death with a baseball bat, and the state where neo-Nazi skinheads murdered two African-Americans because of their skin color, and the state where Bob Jones University spews its anti-Catholic bigotry: they're all red too.[11]

Claims of deep national division were standard fare after the 2000 elections, and to our knowledge few commentators have publicly challenged them.[12] On the contrary, the belief in a frac-tured nation continues to be expressed even by high-level political operatives:

---

[10] Terry Mattingly, "'The Map' Spoke Volumes About Our Country's Divisions," *Knoxville News-Sentinel*, December 30, 2000: B2.

[11] Clinton advisor Paul Begala, as quoted in Bob Clark, "As You Were Saying . . . It's Time for Gore's Pit Bull to Practice What He Preaches," *Boston Herald*, November 18, 2000: 16.

[12] For a prominent exception see Robert Samuelson, "Polarization Myths," *Washington Post*, December 3, 2003: A29.

We have two massive colliding forces. One is rural, Christian,
religiously conservative. [The other] is socially tolerant, pro-
choice, secular, living in New England and the Pacific coast.[13]

You've got 80% to 90% of the country that look at each other
like they are on separate planets.[14]

A November 2003 report of the Pew Research Center for the People & the Press led a prominent journalist to comment:

The red states get redder, the blue states get bluer, and the
political map of the United States takes on the coloration of
the Civil War.[15]

While Andrew Kohut, director of the Pew Center, reportedly commented that

. . . the anger level is so high that if the demonstrators of 1968
had felt like this there would have been gunfire in the streets.[16]

And political commentators see a continuation, if not an intensifi-
cation of the culture war as the 2004 election approaches.

The culture war between the Red and Blue Nations has
erupted again—big time—and will last until Election Day next
year. Front lines are all over, from the Senate to the Pentagon

---

13 Republican pollster Bill McInturff, as quoted in "One Nation, Fairly Divisible, Under God,"
Economist, January 20, 2001: 22.
14 Matthew Dowd, Bush reelection strategist. Dowd was explaining why Bush has not tried to expand
his electoral base. Quoted in Ron Brownstein, "Bush Falls to Pre-9/11 Approval Rating," *Los Angeles
Times*, October 3, 2003: A1.
15 E. J. Dionne Jr., "One Nation Deeply Divided," *Washington Post*, November 7, 2003: A31.
16 Quoted in John Leo, "Splitting Society, Not Hairs," *US News and World Report Science & Society*,
December 15, 2003: 66. Kohut may be too young to remember, but there *was* sporadic gunfire in the
streets and on college campuses during the 1960s "time of troubles." We have more to say about the
Pew Report in Chapter 3.

to Florida to the Virginia suburbs where, at the Bush-Cheney '04 headquarters, they are blunt about the shape of the battle: "The country's split 50-50 again," a top aide told me, "just as it was in 2000." Translation: They can't win re-election by wooing the (mostly coastal) Blue states, but only by firing up (mostly noncoastal) Reds.[17]

The election will be a verdict on the determined yet controversial way in which Mr. Bush has steered his country. It also comes at a time when America is more bitterly divided than it has been for a generation.[18]

In sum, contemporary observers of American politics apparently have reached a new consensus around the proposition that old disagreements about economics now pale in comparison to new divisions based on sexuality, morality, and religion, divisions so deep as to justify fears of violence and talk of war in describing them.[19]

This short book advances a contrary thesis: the sentiments expressed in the previously quoted pronouncements of scholars, journalists, and politicos range from simple exaggeration to sheer nonsense. Such assertions both reflect and contribute to a widespread mythology about contemporary American politics. The simple truth is that there is no culture war in the United States— no battle for the soul of America rages, at least none that most

---

[17] Howard Fineman, "Election Boils Down to a Culture War: Abortion Issue is First Skirmish in the Battle for White House." *Newsweek.* October 22, 2003. http://msnbc.msn.com/id/3225677, accessed December 12, 2003.
[18] "America's Angry Election," *Economist*, January 3, 2004: 7.
[19] Of course, there is nothing new about cultural conflict in the United States—it has been a common element of our politics since the beginning of the Republic. It only seems new to today's generation of political commentators because such issues were relatively muted during the 1930s to the 1960s.

Americans are aware of. Certainly, one can find a few warriors who engage in noisy skirmishes. Many of the activists in the political parties and the various cause groups do, in fact, hate each other and regard themselves as combatants in a war. But their hatreds and battles are not shared by the great mass of the American people—certainly nowhere near to "80–90 percent of the country"—who are for the most part moderate in their views and tolerant in their manner.[20] The bulk of the American citizenry is somewhat in the position of the unfortunate citizens of some third-world countries who try to stay out of the crossfire while Maoist guerrillas and right-wing death squads shoot at each other.

The myth of a culture war rests on misinterpretation of election returns, lack of hard examination of polling data, systematic and self-serving misrepresentation by issue activists, and selective coverage by an uncritical media more concerned with news value than with getting the story right. There is little evidence that Americans' ideological or policy *positions* are more polarized today than they were two or three decades ago, although their *choices* often seem to be. The explanation is that the political figures Americans evaluate are more polarized. A polarized political class makes the citzenry appear polarized, but it is only that—an appearance.

In Chapter 2 we show that the red state versus blue state contrast grossly exaggerates the actual differences among their residents. Chapter 3 shows that the United States is not polarized along other traditional cleavage lines either. What has happened is

---

[20] Thus, our conclusions support the earlier findings of Alan Wolfe, *One Nation, After All* (New York: Viking, 1998). In some circles Wolfe's findings have been discounted as reflecting only the views of 200 middle class suburban families. The chapters that follow report similar findings based on an examination of the views of tens of thousands of Americans questioned in national surveys.

that partisans have become better sorted into the parties than in past decades. Thus, at the highest levels the parties are more polarized, but most commentators fail to realize that this *partisan* polarization has only a faint reflection in *popular* polarization, so the latter certainly is not a cause of the former. Chapter 4 shows that the picture of a largely centrist population holds even when we focus on abortion. Chapter 5 addresses a rapidly changing subject—attitudes toward homosexual rights—that exploded on the national scene in the form of the gay marriage issue in the spring of 2004. While there is considerable division in the population about gay rights and gay marriage, the movement toward increased acceptance of gays and lesbians in the past decade has been so strong that we believe the present divisions are largely a transitional state. Chapter 6 shows that the purported replacement of economic cleavages in the electorate by religious ones is a premature conclusion. Chapter 7 shows how the polarization of partisan elites can give the *appearance* that voters are shifting emphasis from economics to religion and morality, even while voter preferences change not a whit. Finally, Chapter 8 discusses how extreme voices have come to dominate American political discourse, and how their influence might be lessened and the vast middle ground empowered.

CHAPTER 2

A 50:50 Nation?
The Red and the Blue States

In one of the claims quoted in the preceding chapter a writer for the *Economist* refers to "the 50:50 nation." During the late 1990s and early 2000s this phrase began to appear in popular discussions of American politics, as did a similar phrase, "the 49 percent nation."[1] Such phraseology referred to the closely divided national elections of the late 1990s, when the winning party's popular vote share repeatedly came in right around 49 percent of the total vote:

- 1996 Clinton Vote   49.2%
- 1996 Republican House Vote   48.9
- 1998 Republican House Vote   48.9
- 2000 Gore Vote   48.4

---

[1] Michael Barone, "The 49% Nation," in Michael Barone, Richard Cohen, and Charles E. Cook Jr., eds., *The Almanac of American Politics* (Washington, DC: National Journal, 2002): 21–45.

- 2000 Republican House Vote   48.3
- 2002 Republican House Vote   50.9

If we consider only the two-party vote, the parties are almost exactly evenly matched nationally—50:50—or at least they were until the 2002 House elections, when the Republicans broke through that ceiling and got to 52.9 percent. Clearly, recent national elections have been exceedingly close. No presidential candidate has won a majority of the popular vote since 1988, the past three elections constituting the longest such streak since the so-called "era of indecision," when no presidential candidate won a majority of the popular vote in the four elections from 1880 to 1892.

The question is what to make of these recent close elections? For most commentators, the answer is obvious: the American electorate is polarized. In the previously quoted words of the *Economist,* the close recent U.S. elections ". . . *reflect deep demographic divisions. . . . The 50-50 nation appears to be made up of two big, separate voting blocks, with only a small number of swing voters in the middle."* The top panel of Figure 2.1 depicts this claim graphically. The electorate is highly polarized: a large number of "progressives" on the left support the Democrats, a large number of "orthodox" on the right support the Republicans, and very few people occupy the middle ground. With a polarized electorate like this, elections will be very close, half the voters will cheer, and half the voters will seethe, as *USA Today* asserts.

But the U-shaped distribution in the top panel of the figure is not the only electoral configuration that will produce close elections. Most obviously, consider the bell-shaped distribution in the

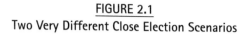

FIGURE 2.1
Two Very Different Close Election Scenarios

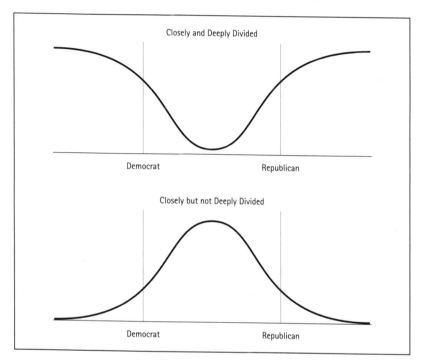

bottom panel of Figure 2.1, which is the inverse of the U-shaped distribution in the top. In the lower figure most people hold moderate or centrist positions and relatively few are extreme partisans. But if the Democratic and Republican parties position themselves equidistant from the center on opposite sides, then the bottom configuration too produces close elections. In both examples the electorate is *closely* divided, but only in the top panel of the figure would we say that the voters are *deeply* divided. In the top panel it would be accurate to say that voters are polarized, but in the bottom panel we would more accurately call most voters ambivalent or indifferent.

When an election results in a near 50:50 outcome, the standard interpretation seems to be that the electorate is polarized as in the top panel of Figure 2.1. Why should that be the default interpretation? When an individual voter reports that he or she is on the fence (50:50) about whom to vote for, everyone understands that there are a number of plausible interpretations: the individual likes both candidates equally, dislikes both candidates equally, or really doesn't give a damn. No one suggests that the individual is polarized. But the aggregate and individual situations are analogous. In each case a continuous variable (percent of the vote/probability of voting for a given candidate) is compressed into a dichotomous variable (Republican or Democratic victory/Republican or Democratic vote), with enormous loss of information. To illustrate, consider the map on the inside back cover of this book, which differs from the red and blue map on the front cover in that a state is colored red or blue only if it was won by a margin of 55:45 or greater, a standard political science definition of marginality. Now a great deal of the map is gray, reflecting the fact that many states are marginal and not securely in the camp of one party or the other. In language analogous to that used to describe individual voters, we might call such states "ambivalent" or "uncertain."

In sum, close elections may reflect equal numbers of voters who hate one candidate and love the other, voters who like both, voters who do not care much at all about either candidate, or various combinations of these conditions. Without taking a detailed look at voter attitudes, we cannot determine whether close elections reflect a polarized electorate that is deeply divided, or an ambivalent electorate that is closely divided between the choices it is offered. So, let us take a closer look at the public opinion that underlies the knife-edge elections of the past few years. Is it as divided as election outcomes seem to suggest?

IS THE COUNTRY POLARIZED?

You've got 80% to 90% of the country that look at each other like they are on separate planets." (Bush reelection strategist, Matthew Dowd).[2]

Is America polarized? Strictly speaking the question should be "has America become *more* polarized?" for that is the claim. But if the country is not polarized to begin with, the question of whether it has become more polarized is moot. Barely two months before the supposed "values chasm separating the blue states from the red ones" emerged in the 2000 election, the Pew Research Center for the People & the Press conducted an extensive national survey that included a wide sampling of issues, a number of those which figure prominently in discussions of the culture war.[3] We have divided the Pew survey respondents into those who resided in states that two months later were to be categorized as blue states and states that two months later were to be categorized as red states. The question is whether there is any indication in these data that the election results would leave one half the country "seething" and one half "cheering," as *USA Today* reports.

---

[2] Quoted in Ron Brownstein, "Bush Falls to Pre-9/11 Approval Rating," *Los Angeles Times*, October 3, 2003: A1.
[3] The Pew survey was conducted August 24–September 10, 2000. Pew's summaries of the findings (along with links to the data and questionnaires) are contained in two separate reports: "Issues and Continuity Now Working for Gore" http://people-press.org/reports/display.php3?ReportID=33 and "Religion and Politics: The Ambivalent Majority" http://people-press.org/reports/display.php3?ReportID=32.

TABLE 2.1
Red Versus Blue States: Political Inclinations

	BLUE	RED
Vote intention: Bush	34%	44%
Democratic self-ID	36	32
Republican self-ID	25	31
Liberal self-ID	22	18
Conservative self-ID	33	41

Table 2.1 indicates that the residents of blue and red states certainly intended to vote differently: the percentage expressing an intention to vote for George Bush was ten points higher in the red states. Reminiscent of our discussion of dichotomous choices, however, the partisan and ideological predispositions underlying these voting differences were less distinct.[4] The difference between the proportions of red and blue state respondents who consider themselves Democrats is not statistically significant, and the difference in the proportions who consider themselves Republicans is barely so—in both red and blue states self-identified independents are the largest group. Similarly, about a fifth of the respondents in both red and blue states consider themselves liberals (the four point difference is not statistically significant), and while there are more conservatives in the red states, there are more conservatives than liberals even in the blue states. In both the red and blue states the largest group of people classified themselves as moderates. In sum, while the aggregate voting patterns of red and blue states

---

[4] More generally, William Mayer shows that in the presidential elections between 1980 and 2000, inclusive, votes are far more polarized than candidate evaluations. See William Mayer, "The Swing Voter in American Presidential Elections: A Preliminary Inquiry," Northeastern University, ms.: Table 2.

TABLE 2.2
Red Versus Blue States: Group Evaluations
(Percent very/mostly favorable toward . . .)

	BLUE	RED
Republican Party	50%	58%
Democratic Party	64	55
Evangelical Christians	60	63
Jews	79	77
Catholics	77	79
Muslims	56	47
Atheists	37	27

would turn out to be quite distinct in November, the underlying patterns of political identification were much less so.

Table 2.2 reports similar results for the group evaluations reported by residents of red and blue states. Unsurprisingly, red state residents regard the Republican Party more favorably than the Democrats, but 55 percent of them regard the Democratic Party favorably. Conversely, blue state residents regard the Democratic Party more favorably than the Republicans, but 50 percent report favorable evaluations of the Republican Party. Evangelical Christians are evaluated equally positively by solid majorities in both red and blue states, as are Jews and Catholics. Muslims fare less well overall and red state residents regard them lower still, but one wonders how much experience many people have with actual Muslims—especially in many of the red states—as opposed to the abstract concept of a Muslim. Finally, in a standard finding, neither red nor blue state residents like atheists: Americans do not

TABLE 2.3
Red Versus Blue States: Beliefs and Perceptions:
(Percent strongly supporting statement)

	BLUE	RED
Gov't almost always wasteful and inefficient	39%	44%
Discrimination main reason blacks cannot get ahead	25	21
Immigrants strengthen our country	44	32
Fight for country right or wrong	35	43
Too much power concentrated in large companies	64	62
Corporations make too much profit	44	43
Al Gore is more liberal than he lets on	55	59
George Bush is more conservative than he lets on	59	57
Wish Clinton could run again (strongly disagree)	51	61

care very much what or how people believe, but they are generally negative toward people who don't believe in anything.

Across a range of other matters, blue and red state residents differ little, if at all. Figures in Table 2.3 indicate that similar proportions regard the government as *almost always* wasteful and inefficient—relative to the red states, the blue states clearly are not wellsprings of support for big government. Only small minorities in either category regard discrimination as the main reason that African Americans can't get ahead—the blue states are not hotbeds of racial liberalism. Immigrants receive a warmer reception among blue state residents, but multiculturalism remains a minority position even in the blue states. Blue state residents are less likely to endorse unqualified patriotism.

On the other hand, red state residents are just as likely as blue state residents to believe that large companies have too much power and to think that corporations make too much profit—the red states are not the running dogs of corporate America. Amusingly, majorities in both red and blue states agree that Al Gore is more of a liberal than he lets on, and that George Bush is more of a conservative than he lets on—they were not fooled by all the talk about "progressives" and "compassionate conservatives." And finally—and counter to suggestions of numerous Democrats after the election—majorities in both red and blue states *strongly* disagree with the proposition that they wish Bill Clinton could run again. Clinton was more favorably regarded in the blue states, but Clinton fatigue by no means was limited to the red states.

When it comes to issue sentiments, Table 2.4 shows that in many cases the small differences we have seen so far become even smaller. Contrary to Republican dogma, red state citizens are equally as unenthusiastic about using the surplus (har!) to cut taxes as blue state citizens. Nearly equal numbers of blue and red state residents think the surplus should be used to pay off the national debt, increase domestic spending, and bolster Social Security and Medicare. Contrary to Democratic dogma, blue state citizens are equally as enthusiastic as red state citizens about abolishing the inheritance tax, giving government grants to religious organizations, adopting school vouchers, and partially privatizing Social Security. Overwhelming majorities in both red and blue states favor providing prescription drugs through Medicare, and solid majorities endorse protecting the environment, whatever it takes. Neither red nor blue state residents attach high priority to increasing defense spending. Looking at this series of issue items, one wonders why anyone would bother separating respondents into red and blue categories—the differences are insignificant.

TABLE 2.4
Red Versus Blue States: Issue Sentiments

	BLUE	RED
Should use the surplus to cut taxes	14%	14%
. . . pay off the national debt	21	23
. . . increase domestic spending	28	24
. . . bolster SS and Medicare	35	38
Favor abolition of inheritance tax	70	72
. . . gov't grants to religious organizations	67	66
. . . school vouchers for low and middle income parents	54	50
. . . partial privatization of SS	69	71
. . . Medicare coverage of prescription drugs	91	92
. . . increasing defense spending	30	37
Do whatever it takes to protect the environment	70	64

But, we have not considered the specific issues that define the culture war. Table 2.5 brings us to the heart of the matter—questions of religion, morality, and sexuality.[5] The proportion of Protestants is significantly higher in the red states, of course, as is the proportion of respondents who report having a "born again" experience. There is a real difference here between the heartland and the coasts. But the significance of this difference fades when we dig deeper. Only a minority of red state respondents reports being very involved in church activities—only marginally more than those blue state respondents who report heavy involvement. A higher proportion of red state respondents report that religion is

---

[5] Unfortunately, there was no question about abortion views in the Pew Survey, only an item on "which party would better represent your views?" Such items are contaminated by projection and rationalization. We deal with the question of abortion at length in Chapter 4.

TABLE 2.5
Red Versus Blue States: Religion and Morals

	BLUE	RED
Protestant	50%	69%
"Born again" or Evangelical Christian	28	45
Very involved in church activities	21	29
Religion is very important in my life	62	74
Churches should keep out of politics	46	43
Ever right for clergy to discuss candidates or issues from the pulpit? (yes)	35	33
Ban dangerous books from school libraries (yes)	37	42
Homosexuality should be accepted by society		
Agree strongly	41	31
Agree not strongly	16	14

very important in their lives, but a healthy 62 percent majority of blue state respondents feel similarly. Very similar proportions think churches should stay out of politics, and the minority of red state residents who approve of the clergy talking politics from the pulpit is slightly smaller than the minority in the blue states. Book-burners are only slightly more common in the red states. Finally, there is a clear difference in one of the major issues of the culture war, homosexuality, but probably less of a difference than many would have expected. The level of support for societal acceptance of homosexuality is ten percentage points higher in the blue states (twelve points if we add those who waffle to those who fully accept homosexuality). The difference is statistically significant, but it hardly conjures up an image of two coalitions of deeply opposed states engaged in a culture war. Opinion is almost as divided within the red and the blue states as it is between them. Significantly, this ten- to twelve-point difference on the issue of homosexual acceptance is about as large a difference as we found between red and blue state respondents in the survey. Readers can judge for themselves whether differences of this magnitude justify the military metaphors usually used to describe them.

A legitimate objection to the preceding comparisons is that they include all citizens rather than just voters. Only about half of the age-eligible electorate goes to the polls in contemporary presidential elections, and far fewer vote in lower-level elections. It is well known that partisanship and ideology are strong correlates of who votes: more intense partisans and more extreme ideologues are more likely to vote.[6] Thus, it is possible that the *voters* in red states differ more from the *voters* in blue states than the residents do. To consider this possibility we turn to the 2000 National Election Study which—after the election—asks individuals whether and how they voted. In 2000, the NES reported a vote distribution reasonably close to the actual national division: 50.6 percent of the respondents reported voting for Gore, 45.5 percent for Bush, and the remainder for minor candidates.[7]

Tables 2.6 and 2.7 report differences among reported voters in the NES that are only marginally larger than those reported among all respondents in the Pew Survey. Again, the largest difference is for the vote itself. To reiterate, even if an individual feels 55:45 between the two candidates, she has to vote one way or the

6 For time series data see Figures 2a–2b and 3a–3b in Morris Fiorina, "Whatever Happened to the Median Voter?" available at http://www.stanford.edu/~mfiorina/.
7 http://www.umich.edu/~nes/. The National Election Studies is a research and data-distribution organization located at the University of Michigan and supported by the National Science Foundation. Surveys have been conducted in every national election year since 1952.

TABLE 2.6
Red Versus Blue States: Political Inclinations

	BLUE	RED
Bush vote	37%	54%
Democratic self-ID*	40	32
Republican self-ID	25	34
Liberal self-ID	20	11
Conservative self-ID	24	31
Clinton job approval**	71	57
Clinton foreign policy job approval	70	63
Clinton economic job approval	81	74
Democrats better able to handle economy	35	27
Republicans better able to handle economy	24	29
Prefer unified control	24	24

* Party identifiers include strong and weak identifiers, not independent leaners.
  Liberal identifiers are scale positions 1–2, conservative identifiers 6–7.
**Unless otherwise noted approval figures in the table combine "strongly approve"
  and "approve."

other. The reported vote for Bush is 54 percent in the red states versus 37 percent in the blue states—a seventeen-point gap, which is larger than the ten-point gap in vote *intention* in the earlier Pew Survey. Self-identified Democrats were significantly more common among blue state voters and self-identified Republicans significantly more common among red state voters, but in neither case does the difference reach double digits; independents and minor party affiliates were a third of the actual electorate in both categories. Self-identified liberals are more common in the blue states, but self-identified conservatives were at least as numerous as liberals in blue states. Again, moderates or centrists were the majority in both categories. An overwhelming majority of blue state voters approved of Bill Clinton's general job performance as well as his foreign policy job performance and his economic job performance, but so did a heavy, if smaller, majority of red state voters. Only minorities of both blue state and red state voters thought that one party could better handle the economy. Finally, rather than blue state residents favoring Democratic control of the Presidency and Congress and red state residents favoring Republican control, nearly identical majorities of both prefer divided control.

Table 2.7 indicates that issue preferences in the two categories of states are surprisingly similar in many instances. Four in ten voters in both red and blue states agree that immigration should decrease, and seven in ten believe that English should be the official language of the United States (the proportion is actually slightly higher in the blue states). Four in ten voters in both categories put environmental considerations above employment considerations, a surprising similarity in light of the image of red states as hotbeds of clear-cutters and blue states as strongholds of tree-huggers. Narrow majorities of voters in both categories support school vouchers, and large majorities support the death penalty. In neither blue nor red states are people wildly in favor of government intervention to ensure fair treatment of African Americans in employment, and virtually identical (small) proportions support racial preferences in hiring.

Again, when we turn to the specific issues that define the culture war, larger differences emerge, but there also are numerous surprises. A solid majority of blue state voters support stricter gun control laws, but so does a narrow majority of red state voters. Support for women's equality is overwhelming and identical among

TABLE 2.7
Red Versus Blue States: Issue Preferences

	BLUE	RED
Immigration should decrease*	41%	43%
Make English official language	70	66
Environment over jobs	43	42
Favor school vouchers	51	54
Favor death penalty	70	77
Government should ensure fair treatment of blacks in employment	57	51
Blacks should get preferences in hiring	13	14
Stricter gun control	64	52
Equal women's role**	83	82
Attend church regularly	50	65
Moral climate: much worse	26	30
somewhat worse	25	25
Tolerate others' moral views	62	62
Abortion—always legal	48	37
Allow homosexual adoption	52	40
No gay job discrimination	73	62
Favor gays in military (strongly)	60	44

* Unless otherwise noted, the figures in the table combine "strongly" or "completely agree" responses with "mostly" or "somewhat agree" responses
**Scale positions 1–2

voters in both categories of states. Although regular church attenders are significantly more common in the red states, similar proportions in both red and blue states believe the moral climate of the country has deteriorated since 1992, and identical proportions believe that others' moral views should be tolerated. Support for unrestricted abortion is eleven points higher among blue state voters, but such unqualified support falls short of a majority, and more than a third of red state voters offer similarly unqualified support. The 2000 NES is particularly rich in items tapping people's views about matters related to sexual orientation. Here we find differences between blue and red state voters that are statistically significant, though smaller in magnitude than regular consumers of the news might have expected. A narrow majority of blue state voters would allow homosexuals to adopt children, but so would four in ten red state voters. Solid majorities of voters in both categories support laws that would ban employment discrimination against gays. Sixty percent of blue state voters fully support gays in the military, contrasted with 44 percent of red state voters. This 16 percent difference is the single largest disparity we found between the issue preferences of red and blue state voters. Perhaps Bill Clinton picked the one issue in the realm of sexual orientation that was most likely to create controversy. But the evidence supports the alternative hypothesis that Clinton's executive order polarized the electorate: according to Gallup data, popular support for gays in the military rose through the 1980s and had reached 60 percent in 1989 before plummeting in the wake of Clinton's executive order.[8]

All in all, the comparison of blue and red state residents who claim to have voted in 2000 seems consistent with the picture reflecting comparisons of all residents of blue and red states. There are numerous similarities between red and blue state voters, some differences, and a few notable differences, but little that calls to mind the portrait of a culture war between the states.

---

[8] Alan Young, "Poll Trends—Attitudes Toward Homosexuality," *Public Opinion Quarterly* 61 (1997): 502.

RED STATES VERSUS BLUE STATES: A SUMMARY

Since 1972 the National Election Studies have included an item that asks respondents to place themselves on a seven-category liberal-conservative scale that runs from "extremely liberal" on the left to "extremely conservative" on the right. If the "two nations" metaphor accurately describes the electorate, red state residents should overwhelmingly position themselves on the right of the scale, and blue state residents on the left. Figure 2.2 compares the ideological distributions of red and blue state residents (top panel) and voters (bottom panel).[9] As seen, the distributions of self-placements in the red and blue states are very similar—both are centered over the "moderate" or "middle-of-the road" position, whether we consider all residents or just voters.[10] Moreover, as Figure 2.3 shows, the respondents in red and blue states are in almost complete agreement about the positions of the two parties: large pluralities place the Democratic Party at scale position 2 ("liberal"), and majorities place the Republican Party at scale position 6 ("conservative"). When combined with the data presented earlier in this chapter we think the evidence is compelling that the bottom panel of Figure 2.1 (p. 13) better describes the current state of American politics than the top panel. Elections are close, but voters are not deeply or bitterly divided. In both red

---

[9] Figures 2.2 and 2.3 are based on the half of the 2000 sample that received the traditional seven-point scale. Because of a question wording experiment the other half of the sample received a branching format question.

[10] We omit those respondents who reply that they do not think of themselves in these terms or do not know what they are—generally about 30 percent of the sample. Political scientists often add this group to those in the middle scale position, which, of course, would make the case for a centrist electorate even stronger.

FIGURE 2.2
Both Red and Blue State Residents Are Basically Centrists

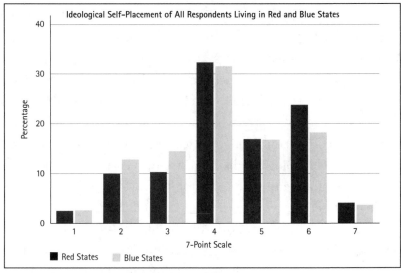

Source: Calculated from the 2000 National Election Studies.

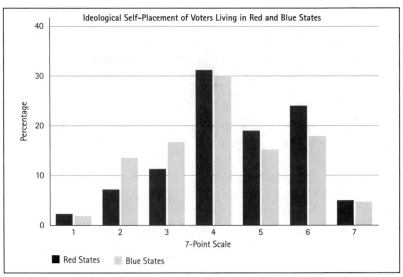

Source: Calculated from the 2000 National Election Studies.

FIGURE 2.3
Red and Blue State Residents Agree That the Parties Are Not Centrist

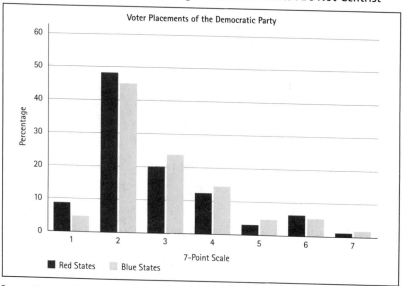

Source: Calculated from the 2000 National Election Studies.

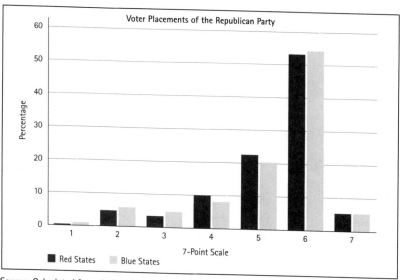

Source: Calculated from the 2000 National Election Studies.

and blue states a solid majority of voters see themselves as positioned between two relatively extreme parties.

THE OBVIOUS HYPOTHESIS

Given the surprisingly small differences between red and blue states that are apparent in survey data, what underlies all the discussion about the clash of cultures? The most plausible explanation is that culture wars, two nations, and similar exaggerations make an excellent story line for the media, so differences are systematically exaggerated to support the story line. Consider an extensive follow-up report on the 2000 elections published in *USA Today*.[11] Rather than conduct a comprehensive examination of representative survey data, *USA Today* chose two towns—Montclair, New Jersey, and Franklin, Tennessee—to exemplify the cultural differences assumed to exist between the red and blue states. The three-day report discussed public opinion in the towns and reported in detail on the residents and their views. The resulting profile painted a vivid portrait of an America deeply divided by both values and lifestyle.

Montclair, where Gore got three-quarters of the vote, is described as a bustling suburb. With jazz clubs, art museums, and coffee bars it is "teeming with energy and interaction." According to the profile, the local interest groups and associations are prominently left of center: "Montclair has its own gun control, abortion rights, and antiwar groups, its own chapters of Amnesty International and the NAACP." The Council for Secular Humanism recently opened up a "faith-free" Center for Inquiry.

---

11 http://pqasb.pqarchiver.com/USAToday/results.html?num=25&st=basic&QryTxt=One+Nation—Divided&sortby=REVERSE_CHRON&datetype=7&x=21&y=10.

In contrast, Franklin, Tennessee, where Bush won by almost thirty points, has brick buildings on Main Street and "shops with such names as Pigg & Peach and Heart and Hands." A Confederate war memorial stands on the town square. The Christian music industry is prominent, with gospel music associations looking for space in the town. Franklin's interest groups and associations are right-leaning: "It's home to the Middle Tennessee Home Education Association for home-schoolers and Christian World Broadcasting, which produces Christian programming in Russian and Chinese and beams it to those countries from a tower in Alaska." The local colleges are mostly Christian.[12]

USA Today went to some length to highlight differences between the two towns. When it came to gun control, for example, USA Today interviewed a gun control activist in Montclair, the father of a young man left permanently crippled by a Palestinian terrorist shooter on the Empire State Building observation deck. His views were contrasted with the views of the owner of the Franklin Gun Shop. In all likelihood readers remember vivid contrasts like these—however extreme and unrepresentative—much longer than marginal differences in nationally representative polls, such as those presented earlier in this chapter.

In sum, rather than draw the conclusion that the country is deeply divided from a systematic look at a broad array of data, USA Today reversed the process, selecting data to fit its preexisting conclusion that the country was deeply divided. USA Today is a reputable national newspaper, more balanced in its political coverage than other national newspapers (one of us even is a long-term subscriber—its graphics are valuable teaching aids). Thus, it

---

[12] Jill Lawrence, "One Nation, Divided" USA Today, February 18, 2002: 10A.

pains us to give *USA Today* an "F" on this report, although we hasten to add that it is not atypical of what one finds in the media.[13] Repeatedly subjected to "analyses" like this one, people can hardly be blamed for believing in a culture war between the states—at least those who play attention to politics.[14] We have read a great deal of popular commentary on the red and blue states and in our view the journalistic analysis that best reflects the statistical portrait we have painted is contained in David Brooks's sensitive contrast of life in Montgomery County, Maryland, with life in Franklin County, Pennsylvania. Our conclusion mirrors his: *"Although there are some real differences between Red and Blue America, there is no fundamental conflict. There may be cracks, but there is no chasm."*[15]

---

13 As this book was going to press, the *Washington Post* published a series of articles on the red and the blue states which made *USA Today's* analysis look comprehensive by comparison. See David Von Drehle, "Political Split is Pervasive," *Washington Post,* April 25, 2004: A1. David Finkel, "For a Conservative, Life is Sweet in Sugar Land, Tex.," *Washington Post,* April 26, 2004: A1. David Finkel, "A Liberal Life in the City by the Bay," *Washington Post,* April 27, 2004: A1.

14 We doubt that the notion of a culture war extends any deeper than the journalistic community and the political class in this country. On numerous occasions when we have tried to describe the research question addressed in this book to neighbors, relatives, and friends, the reaction has been incomprehension. The idea of a culture war is something completely unfamiliar to most Americans.

15 "One Nation, Slightly Divisible," *The Atlantic,* December 2001: 65.

CHAPTER 3

A 50:50 Nation? Beyond the Red and the Blue States

Despite the attention the red state/blue state categorization has received in the media, few professional analysts would be surprised by the lack of major differences in the preceding chapter's contrasts of public opinion in the red and blue states. A state is a large aggregation, a gross unit of comparison. California is a blue state, but as the map (on page 34) of county election returns shows, most of the state's counties are red. Similarly, Texas is a red state, but there is considerable blue in its large cities and along its border with Mexico. For this reason, we doubt that many professional analysts have taken the red states/blue states distinction very seriously. Thus, one can accept the argument that the division of the country into red and blue is a gross exaggeration but still believe that the country is polarized, increasingly so. We simply need to examine other, more precisely defined categories or dimensions in order to find the expected polarization.

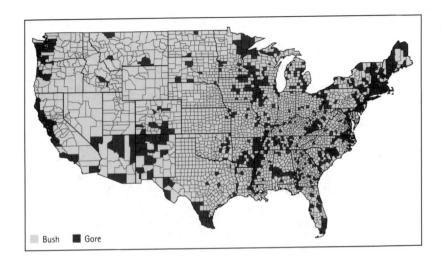

Bush   Gore

IS THE COUNTRY POLARIZED?
DEMOGRAPHIC AND POLITICAL GROUPS

Happily, we need not bury the reader beneath an avalanche of additional data, for there has been some very thorough research on this subject. DiMaggio, Evans, and Bryson have reported an intensive analysis of public opinion covering the period 1972 (when the culture war first flared up) through 1994 (when it erupted into the Republican capture of Congress and Bill Clinton's subsequent impeachment). Evans later updated the study through 2002.[1] Their analysis uses data from the National Election Studies (NES) and the General Social Survey (GSS) and focuses squarely on the question of opinion polarization, applying four different

---

1 Paul DiMaggio, John Evans, and Bethany Bryson, "Have Americans' Social Attitudes Become More Polarized?" *American Journal of Sociology* 102 (1996): 690–775. John Evans, "Have Americans' Attitudes Become More Polarized?—An Update," *Social Science Quarterly* 84 (2003): 71–90.

TABLE 3.1
DiMaggio, Evans, and Bryson
Analysis of Opinion Trends

CHANGE IN OPINION OVER TIME?

By Age—convergence

By Education—convergence

By Race—convergence

By Religion—convergence

By Region—convergence

By Gender—no change

By Ideology—no change (except on abortion)

By Party ID—polarization

---

statistical measures of polarization to thirty-five different opinion scales.[2] Table 3.1 summarizes their findings.

Contrary to claims of growing polarization, DiMaggio, Evans, and Bryson's exhaustive statistical analysis finds that during the last quarter of the twentieth century older and younger Americans grew more alike in their views, not more dissimilar. The same is true for more-well-educated and less-well-educated Americans, for black and white Americans, for Americans of different religious denominations, and for Americans living in different regions. Despite the appearance of a significant gender gap in post-1980 elections, men and women have become neither more nor less similar than in the early 1970s before the gender gap appeared. Americans who self-classify themselves as liberals or conservatives are

---

[2] The NES is discussed in footnote 7 of Chapter 2. The GSS is a continuing study conducted by the National Opinion Research Center at the University of Chicago, partially funded by the National Science Foundation. The survey has been conducted twenty-four times since 1972.

no further apart now than several decades ago, except on the single issue of abortion. The only category that showed evidence of polarization was self-classification by party affiliation: people who consider themselves Democrats and Republicans are further apart in their views than partisans were several decades ago. Overall, DiMaggio and his coauthors conclude that, "The evidence, then, points to dramatic *depolarization* in intergroup differences" (emphasis in original).

What of the possibility that voters polarized before 1972, the starting point of the DiMaggio, Evans, and Bryson study, but political activists and elites did not polarize until later? This possibility is inconsistent with evidence that public opinion tends to lag elite behavior not lead it.[3] Moreover, an earlier report by Glenn finds no evidence of increasing polarization between the early 1950s and late 1960s, although Glenn had fewer measures of opinion available to him than did DiMaggio et al.[4] Ironically, Glenn was searching for evidence of *depolarization* because many at the time thought that the spread of the mass media would have a homogenizing effect on public opinion.

One of the qualifications about the DiMaggio, Evans, and Bryson findings ("no polarization of liberals and conservatives except in the case of abortion") may strike some readers as belonging to the Mrs. Lincoln genre of caveats (Other than that, Mrs. Lincoln, how did you enjoy the play?). If there is a single issue that is the touchstone of the culture war, abortion is it. If there has been significant polarization on abortion, then perhaps

3 For example, Edward Carmines and James Stimson, *Issue Evolution* (Princeton, NJ: Princeton University Press, 1989).
4 Norval Glenn, "Recent Trends in Intercategory Differences in Attitudes," *Social Forces* 52 (1974): 395–401.

it does not matter whether there has been polarization on any other issue. Interestingly, a critique of the DiMaggio, Evans, and Bryson analysis questions the finding of increased polarization on abortion.[5] Mouw and Sobel argue that increasing polarization on the NES abortion question coincides with a change in question wording, suggesting that the finding is an artifact. Moreover, there is evidence that the meaning of individual responses changed with the change in the status quo made by the Supreme Court's *Webster* decision. Mouw and Sobel conclude that

> *Our results indicate no increase in polarization in abortion attitudes between 1980 and 2000. While the contemporary culture wars have been portrayed as a threat to democratic institutions, our evidence suggests that, at least with respect to the debate over abortion rights, the American public is no more divided now than in the past.*[6]

We will have much more to say about abortion in the next chapter.

PARTISAN POLARIZATION

The finding of increasing partisan polarization is consistent with previous academic research and is clearly a significant development.[7] But it is crucial to understand that it is *partisan* polarization, not *popular* polarization. Partisan polarization in the absence

---

[5] Ted Mouw and Michael Sobel, "Culture Wars and Opinion Polarization: The Case of Abortion," *American Journal of Sociology* 106 (2001): 913–43.

[6] Ibid., 938.

[7] For a recent statement see Jon Bond, "Evidence of Increasing Polarization among Ordinary Citizens," in Jeffrey Cohen, Richard Fleisher, and Paul Kantor, eds., *American Political Parties: Decline or Resurgence* (Washington, DC: CQ Press, 2001): 55–77. Some years ago one of us discussed the significance of this development for electoral position-taking. See Morris Fiorina, "Whatever Happened to the Median Voter?" http://www.stanford.edu/~mfiorina/.

of popular polarization indicates that there has been some "sorting" in recent decades—those who affiliate with a party are more likely to affiliate with the "correct" party today than they were in earlier periods. As is widely appreciated, liberal Republicans and conservative Democrats have gotten scarce. The realignment of the South has a lot to do with this, of course. People who once were conservative southern Democrats are now more likely to be conservative southern Republicans, leaving the remaining Democrats more liberal on average and contributing to the increasing conservatism of Republicans. But the South is not the entire story. Research indicates as well that to some extent people are entering the party consistent with their views and to some extent people are changing their views to make them consistent with their party affiliation.[8]

Nevertheless, one should not exaggerate the extent of partisan polarization as did a Pew Research Center report in late 2003. Provocatively titled *The 2004 Political Landscape: Evenly Divided and Increasingly Polarized,* the study received widespread notice in the media.[9] The report was highly informative, summarizing the results of extensive surveys conducted between 1987 and 2003. But despite the claim embodied in the title, one strains to find evidence consistent with increasing polarization in the body of the report or in the myriad tables and figures that accompany the text. For example, the report's first page carries the chart depicted in Figure 3.1 purporting to show a country that is "further apart

---

[8] For recent discussions see Thomas M. Carsey and Geoffrey Layman, "Party Polarization and Party Structuring of Policy Attitudes: A Comparison of Three NES Panel Studies." *Political Behavior*, 24 (2002): 199–236; Geoffrey Layman and Thomas Carsey, "Party Polarization and 'Conflict Extension' in the American Electorate," *American Journal of Political Science* 46 (2002): 786–802.
[9] http://people-press.org/reports/display.php3?ReportID=196.

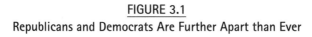

FIGURE 3.1

Republicans and Democrats Are Further Apart than Ever

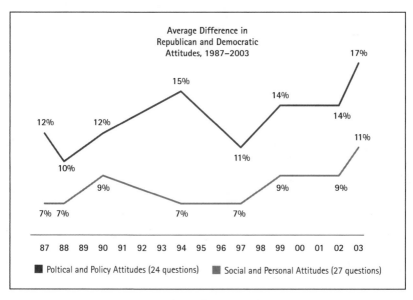

Average Difference in Republican and Democratic Attitudes, 1987–2003

■ Political and Policy Attitudes (24 questions) ■ Social and Personal Attitudes (27 questions)

Source: The Pew Research Center for the People & the Press.

than ever in its political values." Provided that "country" is limited to Democratic and Republican partisans and "ever" means sixteen years, the claim is not exactly false: Democrats and Republicans on average have grown five percentage points further apart in twenty-four political and policy attitudes and four percentage points further apart in seventeen social and personal attitudes between 1987 and 2003. But despite these increases the absolute differences between Democrats and Republicans are relatively small, consistent with those that have been showing up throughout our survey of the evidence. The scale of the Pew figure makes partisan differences look larger than they are, however. Remember

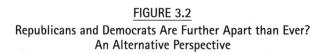

FIGURE 3.2

Republicans and Democrats Are Further Apart than Ever?
An Alternative Perspective

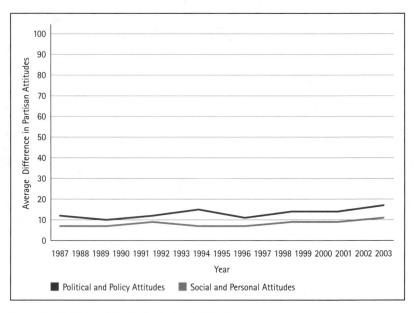

Source: The Pew Research Center for the People & the Press.

that in principle, Democratic and Republican differences could range between 0 percent and 100 percent, as shown in the redrawn plot of the Pew data in Figure 3.2. Rather than "further apart than ever," a glance at Figure 3.2 suggests the far less newsworthy conclusion "still close together but maybe not quite as close as in 1987."

Disaggregation of the Pew scales into their more specific components similarly fails to support the title and tone of the report. For example, two pages after making the claim that Americans are "further apart than ever," the report notes that *"Over the past decade there has been a decided shift across the political spectrum in favor of tolerance on issues relating to homosexuality and race"* (p. 3). And later in the report Pew elaborates on those conclusions: *"Since 1987, Americans—both black and white—have become much more personally tolerant. The idea of blacks and whites dating, once highly divisive, is now broadly accepted. There also has been a steady decline in the number of Americans who say they have little in common with people of other races"* (p. 45). Regarding social issues—the heart of the culture wars, Pew reports that *"Over the past sixteen years, public values on most social issues have remained generally stable. . . . Yet in that period there also has been a distinct shift toward acceptance of several social changes, some of which challenge traditional views of the family"* (p. 69).

In sum, a disinterested reader who plows through the 150+ page report comes away with an impression rather different from the columnist or reporter who reads only the first page.[10] Rather than indicating "further apart than ever," small increases in the size of opinion differences are intermixed with small decreases and numerous fluctuations without any real pattern. Pew is a highly professional organization with an excellent reputation. Thus, the misleading spin they put on their findings attests to the strength and pervasiveness of the prevailing media frame of a polarized nation, a frame that Pew chose to perpetuate rather than use their data to debunk.[11]

---

[10] On a *NewsHour with Jim Lehrer* segment entitled "Divided Nation," former Representative Mickey Edwards commented, "But this poll shows a great deal of division among just registered voters, who are not partisans, not activists. . ." Although that is a defensible rendering of the title and first page of the report, the accompanying data showed no such thing. http://people-press.org/commentary/display.php3?AnalysisID=73.

[11] Pew would have done better to give its report the subtitle of an earlier report: "An Ambivalent Majority."

To continue with the argument offered at the end of the last chapter, the inaccurate picture of national polarization presented by the media undoubtedly reflects the fact that the thin stratum of elected officials, political professionals, and party and issue activists who talk to the media are indeed more distinct, more ideological, and more polarized than those of a generation ago. To a lesser extent the same is true for the strongest identifiers in each party. But the polarization story is much less accurate for the less strongly identified, let alone for political independents and in general for the mass of citizens who rarely are considered worthy of attention from the media, a point that will be strikingly illustrated in the next chapter when we closely examine the abortion issue.

The following three figures illustrate the general pattern. Figure 3.3 depicts the difference in ideological polarization between the 3–5 percent of the citzenry who are party activists, as compared to the 25–30 percent who are strong party identifiers, the 35–40 percent who are only weakly identified and the 25 percent who profess independence but admit to leaning toward a party.[12] The activists are several times more polarized than everyone else, and there is some indication of increased polarization among the strong party identifiers.[13]

One colleague suggested that measures of emotional feeling might show more evidence of increasing polarization than measures of ideological position. The NES includes a device called the "feeling thermometer" which invites respondents to rate individuals and political groupings on a "very cold" to "very warm" scale.

---

[12] The remaining 10 percent of Americans deny any leaning toward either party.
[13] The apparent decline in activist polarization in 2000 is probably only sampling error. Only half of the 2000 NES sample was asked the traditional seven-point scale which resulted in only 33 Democrats being classified as activists. For some reason they were more moderate than usual.

FIGURE 3.3

Partisan Polarization on the Liberal–Conservative Scale Has Not Increased Much in the Past Generation

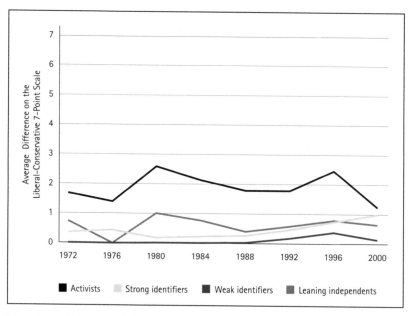

Source: Calculated from the National Election Studies. Activists are defined as party identifiers who report engaging in three or more (of five possible) campaign activities. Party ID measures do not include activists.

If we compare the difference between ratings of one's own party and ratings of the opposing party (Figure 3.4) we find that there has been little increase in polarization since 1980. Strong partisans are far more polarized than weak partisans and independent leaners, but there is only a slight indication of any growing polarization during the past two decades.[14]

---

[14] Interestingly, activists are not quite as favorable to their party and hostile to the other as strong partisans. We have no explanation for this slight difference.

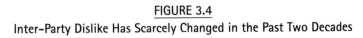

FIGURE 3.4

Inter-Party Dislike Has Scarcely Changed in the Past Two Decades

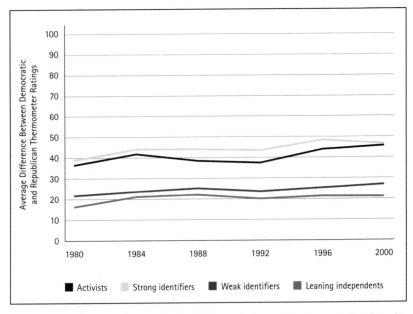

Source: Calculated from the National Election Studies. Activists are defined as party identifiers who report engaging in three or more (of five possible) campaign activities. Party ID measures do not include activists.

If we compare thermometer ratings of liberals and conservatives (Figure 3.5) we find somewhat more evidence of increasing polarization—Democratic activists and strong partisans like liberals and dislike conservatives more than a generation ago, and Republican activists and strong partisans feel just the opposite, but we see the same general pattern of polarization at the top which fades out as partisan commitment declines.[15]

---

[15] See also Evans, "Have Americans' Attitudes Become More Polarized?" Alan Abramowitz and Kyle Saunders, "Ideological Realignment in the U.S. Electorate," *Journal of Politics* 60 (1998) 634–652.

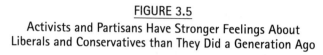

FIGURE 3.5
Activists and Partisans Have Stronger Feelings About Liberals and Conservatives than They Did a Generation Ago

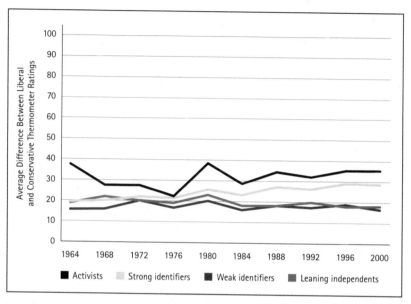

Source: Calculated from the National Election Studies. Activists are defined as party identifiers who report engaging in three or more (of five possible) campaign activities. Party ID measures do not include activists.

IS THE ELECTORATE POLARIZED? INDIVIDUALS

A final objection to our consideration of the relative lack of polarization in the policy preferences of Americans might run something like this: okay, so mass attitudes on political issues are distributed more evenly across states, regions, religions, genders, ages, races, and even parties and ideologies than popular discussions might have led us to believe, but it still may be the case that individual voters are more polarized today than they were a generation ago. The blue/red categorization of the journalists and the classic demographic categories of the social scientists may simply not correlate as highly with policy attitudes today because the natural communities of the past have eroded under the assaults of increased geographic mobility and the revolution in communications technology. Citizens now choose their beliefs with less regard to where they live and who they are than in past decades, but individuals are more polarized, nevertheless.

This is a more difficult objection to consider than simply categorizing people in different ways and comparing their similarities and differences, but an earlier research project of ours enables us to offer a response to the objection. In an analysis that sought to explain Al Gore's surprisingly poor showing in 2000 we estimated vote choice models for all voters in the elections between 1972 and 2000.[16] The data were drawn from the National Election Studies, and the estimated models incorporated identical survey items asked in each of the eight presidential studies conducted during the period. Vote predictors included party affiliation, ideological self-classification, presidential performance judgments, evaluations of the two major candidates, and evaluations of economic conditions in the country. The statistical output of the estimated equations consists of probabilities that the voter would support the Republican or Democratic candidate.[17]

Now, if voters have become more polarized over time we should see an increase in the number of voters predicted to vote

---

[16] Morris Fiorina, Samuel Abrams, and Jeremy Pope, "The 2000 US Presidential Election: Can Retrospective Voting Be Saved?" *British Journal of Political Science* 33 (2003): 163–187.
[17] The estimation method was probit analysis. It generates predicted probabilities of voting for Bush versus Gore, which are the basis of the figure.

for one candidate with very high probability and the other candidate with very low probability, or equivalently, a decrease in voters with probabilities of voting for the two candidates that are close to 50:50. Since there is no generally agreed-upon definition of what is very high probability, we present the results for three increasingly strict definitions: 70:30, 80:20, and 90:10. As shown in Figure 3.6 the exact definition of polarization makes little difference. Taking a strict definition of polarization (90:10) we see that about 60 percent of the electorate was polarized in the 1972–1980 elections, a figure that increased 10–15 percent in the Reagan-Clinton years, but then *declined* in 2000. The same

FIGURE 3.6
Levels of Individual Voter Polarization

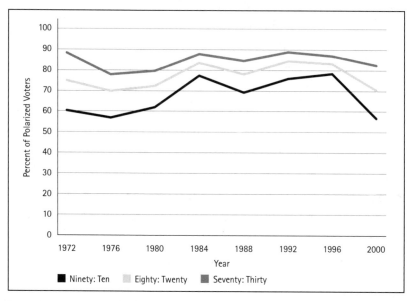

Source: Calculated from the National Election Studies.

pattern holds with less strict definitions of polarization—a rise in the Reagan-Clinton years, but a drop in 2000. On the whole the estimated levels of individual voter polarization are relatively high overall, but polarization in 2000 is about the same as in the Ford-Carter election of 1976. Like the 2000 election that was a very close election, but in contrast to the commentary surrounding 2000, we do not recall much talk of how polarized the country was in 1976.

SUMMARY: NOT A POLARIZED ELECTORATE

To some degree, polarization is a subjective judgment. For some people a 10 percent difference in the preferences of a state or a socioeconomic group on abortion or gay rights may be sufficient to conclude that the American electorate is engaged in a culture war. Our judgment differs. Certainly, in a majority rule electoral system 10 percent differences that occur in the neighborhood of 50 percent may be politically very consequential. A jurisdiction with a small right-of-center majority may elect a hard-right Republican representative while another with a small left-of-center majority may elect a hard-left Democrat. But to infer from the polarization of election outcomes that voters in the first jurisdiction overwhelmingly disagree with voters in the second jurisdiction is both a logical error and an inference at odds with the data.

On the contrary, the data presented in this and the preceding chapter indicate that reports of an American population polarized around moral and religious issues—or any other issue for that matter—are greatly exaggerated. That is especially true for the red/blue state categorization so popular in the contemporary media, but it is true as well when one looks at traditional demographic categories dear to the hearts of sociologists and political scientists. Even taking the analysis down to the level of individual voters reveals that while a majority of Americans go to the polls with a fairly set idea of how they will cast their votes, that majority was no bigger in 2000 than in 1976. Reports of a culture war are mostly wishful thinking and useful fund-raising strategies on the part of culture war guerrillas, abetted by a media driven by the need to make the dull and everyday appear exciting and unprecedented.

In one of its articles on the 50:50 nation the *Economist* remarked in passing that a misprint in one draft had rendered the phrase, the "so-so nation." Unintentional though it was, that misprint better describes the state of American public opinion than do the commentaries of many political pundits.

A PUZZLE

But if Americans are about as liberal or conservative as they were a generation ago, if their positions on specific issues have not polarized, and if partisan polarization has increased, although not by as much as often assumed, how can we explain the polarized *choices* reported by many polls in the spring of 2004? Polls are reporting that up to 90 percent of Republicans approve of President Bush's performance while similar proportions of Democrats disapprove. Trial heats report comparable partisan divisions, with 90 percent of Republicans intending to vote for Bush and 90 percent of Democrats for Kerry. The answer is that it is not voters who have polarized, but the candidates they are asked to choose between. Consider a number of thought experiments: (1) Would presidential performance numbers be so polarized if George Bush had never launched a war on Iraq, never proposed drilling in the Arctic Wildlife Refuge, and never advocated a constitutional amendment outlawing gay marriage, to name a few controversial actions and proposals? (2) Would presidential performance numbers be so polarized if John McCain were president? (3) Would the trial heat numbers be so polarized if the presidential nominees were Senator John McCain and Senator Joseph Lieberman? We believe that the answer to all three questions is no: polarized alternatives can produce the *appearance* of polarized citizens. More on this in Chapter 7.

CHAPTER 4

A Closer Look at Abortion

In 1973 the Supreme Court decided *Roe* v. *Wade*, striking down any restrictions on a woman's right to terminate a pregnancy in the first trimester and limiting restrictions on that right in the second trimester. In the intervening three decades abortion has remained on the national agenda, and many observers regard it as the defining issue in the culture wars. Luker describes how the right-to-life movement grew in reaction to the *Roe* decision.[1] And, more broadly, there is little doubt that antiabortion activism was an important component of the development of the religious right in the 1970s. The religious right, of course, defines the "orthodox" position in the purported culture wars.

For a subject that has been so much studied and discussed there are a surprising number of major misconceptions about public attitudes toward abortion. Indeed, to a considerable extent the general myth of a culture war probably rests on several more specific myths

---

[1] Kristin Luker, *Abortion and the Politics of Motherhood* (Berkeley, CA: University of California Press, 1984).

about public opinion on abortion. For example, we are often told that the country is polarized on the issue of abortion. This claim is false. Similarly, we often hear the related claim that abortion is an issue that is not susceptible to compromise. This claim too is false—at least from the standpoint of the great majority of Americans. Finally, we often hear and read that because of the parties' stands on abortion a gender gap has developed, wherein women disproportionately support the pro-choice Democratic Party while men disproportionately support the pro-life Republican Party. Again, this claim is false: the gender gap is real, of course, but contrary to popular commentary, it has little or nothing to do with abortion. We hasten to add that we are not telling disinterested analysts of public opinion anything new here, but there is a large gap between what academic analysts know to be fact and what political debate and media commentary depict as fact.[2]

PUBLIC ATTITUDES TOWARD ABORTION: "I'M 'PRO-CHOICE,' BUT . . ."

As with most topics in public opinion polling, question wording makes a great deal of difference in how people respond to questions about abortion, a fact that is naturally exploited by both the pro-choice and pro-life sides of the debate. The antiabortion side emphasizes the act of aborting a fetus. Polls consistently show that many Americans are troubled by abortion; indeed, as Table 4.1 shows about as many respondents in national surveys opine that

---

[2] For an excellent earlier survey of public opinion on abortion see Elizabeth Cook, Ted Jelen, and Clyde Wilcox, *Between Two Absolutes* (Boulder, CO: Westview Press, 1992).

TABLE 4.1
Is Abortion Murder?

"Some people say that abortion is an act of murder, while other people disagree with this. What is your view—do you think that abortion is an act of murder or don't you feel this way?"

	ACT OF MURDER	DON'T FEEL THIS WAY
January 1995	40%	51%
January 1998	48	45
January 2003	46	46

Source: Everett Ladd and Karlyn Bowman, *Public Opinion About Abortion*. Washington, DC: AEI Press, 2nd ed. 2000: 26. The 2003 figure supplied by Karlyn Bowman. The original data are taken from surveys using identical question wording by Yankelovich, Gallup, and Harris/CNN/Time, respectively.

abortion is murder as deny that it is.[3] But—and this is a critically important point—not everyone who believes that abortion is wrong—not even everyone who believes it is murderous—supports making it illegal. For, just as consistently, over the past fifteen years national polls report that a majority of Americans believe in the principle of choice, and support for *Roe* now approaches the two-thirds majority level (Figure 4.1).[4] The juxtaposition of these two findings logically implies that a significant number of people who believe that abortion is wrong nevertheless support the principle of a woman's right to choose as embodied in *Roe*.

There is no necessary logical inconsistency here, of course; many people may simply decline to impose their personal views on the rest of society, a subject we return to in a later chapter. Nor does the juxtaposition of pro-choice with anti-abortion attitudes

---

[3] Surveys by other polling organizations using slightly different question wordings report very similar findings. See Grew Shaw, "Poll Trends: Abortion," *Public Opinion Quarterly*, 67 (2003): 415.

[4] Other polling organizations sometimes report lower support for *Roe* than does Gallup, but almost invariably they report a comfortable majority of Americans in support. Ibid: 426.

FIGURE 4.1

A Clear Majority of Americans Now Support *Roe v. Wade*

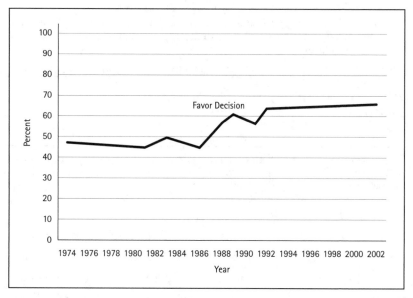

Source: The Gallup Poll.

mean that Americans are confused or uncertain about abortion as they are about some complex technical issues. As noted, abortion has been on the agenda for some three decades and there is reason to believe that most Americans long ago decided where they stood on the issue. When the *same* survey question is repeated over time, public opinion is strikingly stable. The General Social Survey has included the following item for three decades:

> *Please tell me whether or not you think it should be possible for a pregnant woman to obtain a legal abortion if*
>
> 1. *the woman's health is seriously endangered*
> 2. *she became pregnant as a result of rape*

3. *there is a strong chance of serious defect in the baby*
4. *the family has low income and cannot afford any more children*
5. *she is not married and does not want to marry the man*
6. *she is married and does not want any more children*

This item omits any reference to the emotionally charged rhetoric of the abortion debate and focuses purely on the substance of people's beliefs. Figure 4.2 shows that after moving in a liberal

FIGURE 4.2
Popular Attitudes Toward Abortion Have Been Remarkably Stable Since *Roe v. Wade*

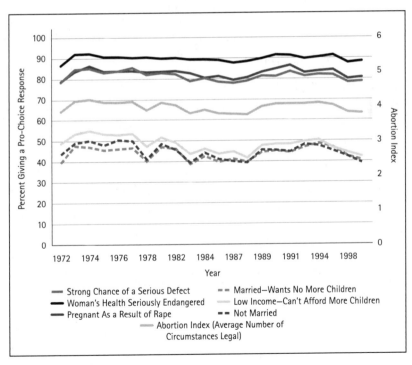

Source: Calculated from the General Social Surveys.

direction in the early 1970s, opinion stabilized at the time of the *Roe* decision, stayed remarkably constant for two decades, and then moved a bit in a conservative direction in the late 1990s.[5] On average, Americans favor legal abortion in about four of the six circumstances, with huge majorities supporting abortion in the first three ("traumatic") circumstances, but bare majorities or only minorities supporting abortion in the second three ("elective") circumstances.[6] Opinion appears to have changed little after the 1989 *Webster* decision, which opened the way for further state regulation of abortion, and after the 1992 *Casey* decision, which upheld some of the specific restrictions imposed by the state of Pennsylvania.

As we would expect, attitudes toward abortion vary across the regions of the country, but the differences are smaller than political commentary would lead the casual reader to expect. As Figure 4.3 shows, in 2000, at the supposed height of the culture war, residents of the red states supported legal abortion in about 3.5 of the six circumstances, a bit lower than the national average, while residents of the blue states supported abortion in 4.1 circumstances, a little higher than the national average. As we noted in the preceding chapter, however, this is a gross classification. In particular, the blue states of the northeast and Great Lakes have a heavy Catholic presence and are home to many socially conservative Democrats.

---

[5] As in Figure 4.2, numerous surveys registered a slight downturn in support for legal abortion in the late 1990s. In recent years some pro-life groups have focused attention on an abortion procedure called "intact dilation and extraction" or "partial birth abortion," in which the fetus is destroyed after it has been partially delivered. Pictures and verbal descriptions offered by pro-life groups are quite gruesome, and large majorities of Americans have consistently registered opposition to this particular procedure. Thus, the debate probably sensitized some generally pro-choice Americans to the fact that they have conditional views on the issue, leading to a drop in unqualified support. Perhaps recognizing these sentiments, despite his pro-choice record, Al Gore announced during the 2000 campaign that he would sign a law passed by Congress that banned partial birth abortions.

[6] The terms "traumatic" and "elective" are those commonly used by researchers in the area and are not used here in any evaluative sense.

FIGURE 4.3
Regions Differ Less on Abortion than Commonly Thought

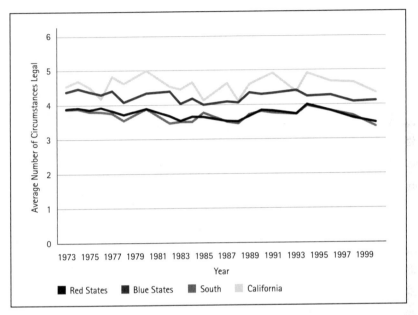

Source: Calculated from the General Social Surveys.

But even if we refine the categories and compare the deep red states of the old confederacy with the quintessential blue state of California, we see surprisingly small differences: citizens of libertine California indeed are on average more pro-choice than citizens of the traditionally minded southern states, but the difference is not zero versus six circumstances, but rather 3.4 versus 4.3. Regional differences are marginal, not major.

Just as regional differences on abortion are smaller than often assumed, so are religious differences. Indeed, Jews are the only group that differs markedly from the national average—most favor legal abortion in all circumstances. As Figure 4.4 shows,

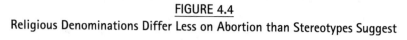

FIGURE 4.4

Religious Denominations Differ Less on Abortion than Stereotypes Suggest

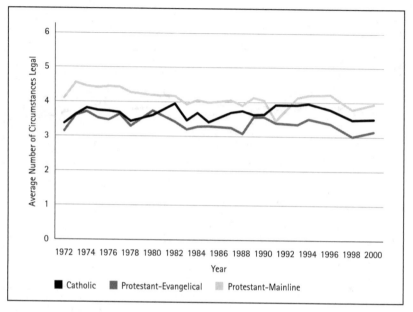

Source: Calculated from the General Social Surveys.

however, Evangelical Protestants differ from mainline Protestants by only about one circumstance out of six, and the average Catholic favors abortion in about 3.5 of the six circumstances. Given that the clergy of the Catholic and Evangelical churches often are portrayed as associated with right-to-life sentiments, it is surprising that their rank-and-file express opinions so close to the center of the issue.

As we will discuss in Chapter 6, in today's world denomination often is less important than religiosity, or a person's degree of religious commitment; hence, Figure 4.4 may understate the connection between religion and abortion attitudes. Figure 4.5 plots

FIGURE 4.5
The Churched and the Unchurched Differ Less on Abortion than Stereotypes Suggest

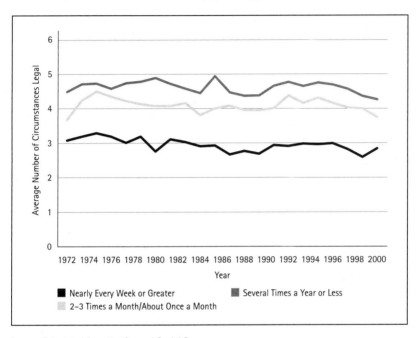

■ Nearly Every Week or Greater   ■ Several Times a Year or Less
■ 2–3 Times a Month/About Once a Month

Source: Calculated from the General Social Surveys.

support for legal abortion as a function of a measure of religious commitment—church attendance—perhaps more revealing than denomination. Again, the figures tend in the expected direction: the unchurched, who rarely attend services, are a bit more pro-choice than the national average, while the believers, who attend services weekly or more, are a full circumstance below the national average. But, again, the difference between the unchurched and the believers is not six circumstances on the scale, or even three or four, but about one and one-half circumstances—not exactly a religious war.

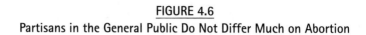

FIGURE 4.6
Partisans in the General Public Do Not Differ Much on Abortion

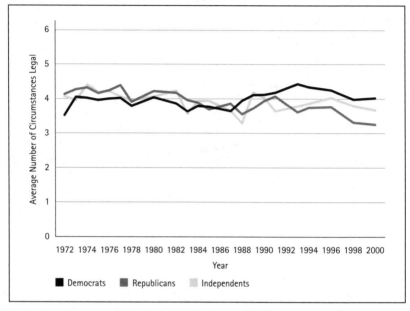

Source: Calculated from the General Social Surveys.
Note: Partisans include strong and weak identifiers.

No doubt Figure 4.6 will surprise many people. The contemporary Democrats indisputably are the party of abortion choice. Democratic presidential candidates must pass a litmus test, and the party even refused to allow the pro-life governor of an electorally important state to speak at the 1996 convention.[7] Just as indisputably the contemporary Republicans are the party of pro-life. Republican presidential candidates must pass a litmus test

---

[7] Robert Casey of Pennsylvania. Richard Gephardt, a pro-life Missouri Baptist, had a pro-choice epiphany before deciding to seek the 1988 Democratic presidential nomination, as did Dennis Kucinich, a pro-life Ohio Catholic before entering the 2004 race for the nomination. Al Gore's conversion (he denies there was one) took place less suddenly. See Walter Robinson and Ann Scales, "Campaign 2000: Gore Record Scrutinized for Veracity," *Boston Globe*, January 28, 2000: A1.

that is the opposite of the Democrats'.[8] Apparently, the word has not gotten out to most of the party rank-and-file, however. As previous analysts have noted, when *Roe* was decided and for some years thereafter, Republicans were ever so slightly more pro-choice than Democrats. Since 1988 self-identified Democrats in the population have been slightly more pro-choice than self-identified Republicans, but the difference has never been more than about three-quarters of a unit on the six-circumstance scale. Given the strong association between the parties' activists and candidates with opposing sides of the abortion issue, the weak differentiation of parties at the mass level is noteworthy.[9]

Because Figure 4.6 is so counter to much of the conventional wisdom it is worthwhile to show that it is not an artifact of the NORC survey question. Figure 4.7 plots the responses of Democrats and Republicans separately for an alternative Gallup survey item that asks simply, "Do you think abortion should be legal under any circumstances, legal only under certain circumstances, or illegal in all circumstances?" A majority of Americans consistently responds "legal only under certain circumstances." Consider the partisan gap in the two more extreme responses chosen by minorities of the population. Beginning in the early 1990s (in response to *Webster?*) a partisan gap of ten to twelve points opened up at the liberal extreme. Democrats are ten to twelve points more likely than Republicans to say "legal under any circumstances," but note that only 30–35 percent of Democrats

---

[8] In 1980 George H. W. Bush was a tolerant New England Episcopalian. By 1988 he was a born-again social conservative. In 1996 plutocrat Steve Forbes was an economic conservative with little interest in social and cultural issues. By the time he again sought the nomination in 2000 he was a committed social conservative.

[9] In Figure 4.6, as elsewhere in this book, strong and weak identifiers are classified as partisans. If independents who lean toward a party are classified as partisans—a coding practice that some political scientists prefer—partisan differences all but disappear.

FIGURE 4.7
When Should Abortion be Legal? Partisans Are Not Very Different

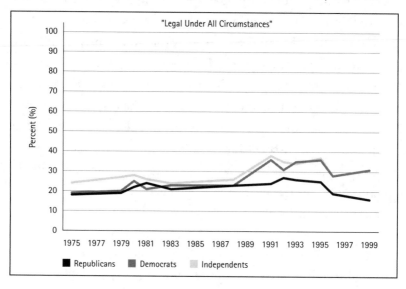

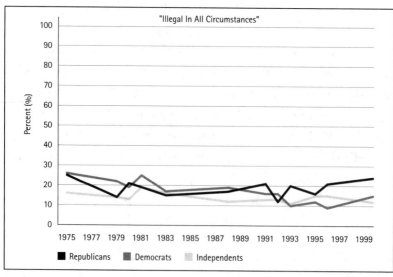

Source: The Gallup Organization.

choose that response. In turn, Republicans are about 5 to 10 points more likely to say "illegal in all circumstances," but only 20–25 percent of Republicans take that position. Depending on the year a little more than 50 percent of Republicans and a little less than 50 percent of Democrats choose "legal only under certain circumstances."

The preceding figures tell a story about American abortion attitudes that differs greatly from the impression one gets from political and media commentary. We hear repeatedly that the Republicans are culturally "orthodox," the party of the right-to-life movement in particular and the religious right in general. The Democrats are culturally "progressive," the party of the right-to-choose movement in particular and secular humanism in general. Such stereotypes have a good deal of validity when describing the parties' office-holders, activists, and associated cause groups, but they are gross exaggerations of differences between the parties' adherents within the broader public.

To be sure, the lack of association between citizens' party affiliations and their views on abortion does not prove that the *labels* "pro-life" and "pro-choice" may have taken on broader connotations, something on the order of "intolerant puritans" on the one hand versus "degenerate libertines" on the other. Thus, voters may be more divided over the labels "pro-life" and "pro-choice" than over actual policy alternatives.[10] But whatever the connotations the labels have taken on, the evidence is clear that the broad American public is not polarized on the specifics of the abortion

---

10 Just as women were more favorable toward government efforts to improve the status of women than they were toward the term "feminist." See "What Women Think about the Feminist Label," *Public Perspective*, November/December 1991: 92–93.

issue. They believe that abortion should be legal but that it is reasonable to regulate it in various ways. They are "pro-choice, buts." Recognizing this state of public opinion, Bill Clinton, one of the most adroit politicians of our era, said that he was pro-choice and against abortion, and we think that Americans understood exactly what he meant.

Americans are traditionally pragmatic, and they approach even an issue like abortion in a pragmatic fashion. They favor the right to choose, but only a small minority favors the right to choose in every conceivable circumstance.[11] Overwhelming majorities regard rape, birth defects, and threats to the mother's life and health as sufficient justifications for abortion, while clear majorities regard personal convenience and gender selection as insufficient. Opinion divides on justifications based on the mother's age, financial condition, and marital status. In this light it was not surprising that at the same time that a two-thirds majority of Americans endorsed *Roe*, about 60 percent of the public also endorsed *Casey* (and Democrats were just as supportive as Republicans), approved of state laws that made abortion more difficult, and opposed public funding of abortion (Tables 4.2 and 4.3). Political folklore holds that the Supreme Court follows the election returns, but in the abortion decisions, it can fairly be said that the Supreme Court followed public opinion, as Justice Scalia complained in his dissent in *Casey*.[12]

---

[11] Moreover, polls probably overestimate the unconditionally pro-choice minority. Bartels reports that in the 1996 NES study about 40 percent reported that they believed a woman should "always be able" to obtain a legal abortion, but in a study the next year, about 40 percent of those same unconditionally pro-choice respondents favored a ban on partial birth abortions and another 12 percent of them were undecided. Many people who unreflectively say "always" or "under any circumstances" don't really believe that when probed. Larry Bartels, "Is 'Popular Rule' Possible?" *Brookings Review* 21 (2003): 14.
[12] *Planned Parenthood of Southeastern Pa. v. Casey* (91-744), 505 U.S. 833 (1992).

TABLE 4.2
Abortion: Post-Casey

As you may know, the Supreme Court recently decided that a woman still has the right to have an abortion until the fetus is viable, but said that certain restrictions—such as a twenty-four hour waiting period, parental consent for girls under eighteen, and requiring doctors to provide information on alternatives to abortion—are legal as long as an undue burden is not placed on a woman seeking an abortion. In general, do you approve or disapprove of the Supreme Court's decision?

Approving:

NATIONAL	59%
Republicans	58%
Democrats	58
Independents	62

Source: *American Viewpoint*, July 8–13, 1992.

TABLE 4.3
Abortion: In Some Circumstances

	OPPOSE	FAVOR
Would you like to see *Roe v. Wade* overturned? (after explanation)	65%	35%
Would you support or oppose the following legislative restriction (except in threat to mother's life):		
Counseling on dangers and alternatives	9	91
Parental permission	23	77
No public funding	36	64
Fetal viability testing	38	62
No public facilities	33	57
No public employees	56	44

Source: Gallup, July 6–7, 1989.

In sum, public opinion on abortion does not support militants on either side of the issue. Militants think in terms of unconditional rights. Pro-choice activists who play an important role in the Democratic Party argue that any infringement on a woman's right to choose is unacceptable, even if that means the occasional abortion of a healthy, near-term fetus. Such people probably comprise less than 10 percent of the population. Pro-life activists who play an important role in the Republican Party argue that any abortion is unacceptable, even if that means the occasional death of a woman. Such people certainly comprise less than 10 percent of the population. The great majority of the American citizenry rejects extreme positions and could be content with compromise laws, but such compromises are hard to achieve given the current state of American electoral politics.[13]

ABORTION AND THE GENDER GAP

Yet another staple of contemporary political commentary is the gender gap in support for the major parties beginning with Ronald Reagan's defeat of Jimmy Carter in 1980. In presidential elections (Figure 4.8) and increasingly in congressional elections, women have voted consistently more Democratic than men, a trend that reached its height—so far—in the 1996 election when the gap between men's and women's support for Bill Clinton

---

[13] Arguably the difficulty of compromising has been greater for the Republicans, many of whose activists are committed to changing a status quo that a majority of the country accepts. See David Brady and Edward Schwartz, "Abortion Politics in the U.S. Senate," *Public Choice* 84 (1995): 25–48. More recently the controversy over partial birth abortion has created greater difficulties for the Democrats. Note that in Europe, where citizen activists and interest groups are less influential relative to party professionals, compromise abortion laws have been much less difficult to adopt than in the United States.

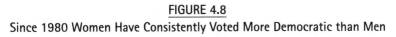

FIGURE 4.8

Since 1980 Women Have Consistently Voted More Democratic than Men

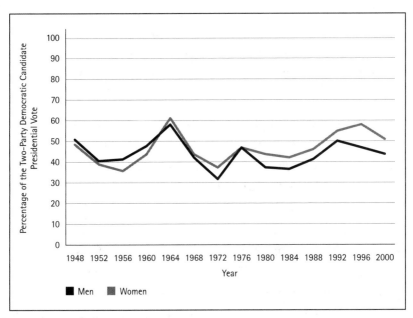

Source: Calculated from the National Election Studies.

reached double digits—almost fifteen points. (Several polls suggested that Robert Dole would have narrowly won the election
had only men voted). Pro-choice groups have seized on the gender
gap to argue that Republicans are out of step with American
women on the issue of abortion, a charge uncritically echoed by
politicians and pundits:

> *Democrats believe women will reject Bush because of his con-
> servative positions on issues such as abortion.*[14]

---

14 Judy Keen, "Bush Is Working to Woo Female Voters," *USA Today*, March 6, 2000: 10A.

In California, the abortion issue holds enormous sway among women who have provided a crucial "gender gap" margin-of-victory vote.[15]

Just as the Christian right created a gender gap by its opposition to abortion, so Dean will trigger a values gap that will send moderate voters flocking in droves to the Republicans.[16]

Here is another myth about American politics. Yes, the gender gap is politically significant. So is the abortion issue. And as we saw in the preceding section, extreme pro-life Republicans *are* out of step with American women on the issue. But they are out of step with men as well, and the same holds for extreme pro-choice Democrats.[17] The simple albeit surprising fact is that the gender gap is not a reflection of differing men's and women's view about abortion: there is no evidence that the abortion issue has anything to do with the gender gap. Claims to the contrary are myth.

Consider Figure 4.9. Evidently, women's and men's attitudes on abortion do not differ either nationally, or in California, where the Republican implosion between the Reagan and Clinton administrations often is attributed to the issue. Public opinion analysts have long known that men and women do not differ on the subject of abortion, and as in Figure 4.9, whatever small differences appear often reflect the fact that men are slightly more

---

[15] Carla Marinucci, "At S.F. Meeting, Pro-Choice GOP Women Lament Their Bitter Dilemma," *San Francisco Chronicle*, March 11, 2000: A3.

[16] Dick Morris, "McGovern II. . ." *New York Post* online edition, July 9, 2003: 2.

[17] Even academics show a tendency to forget their professional training when discussing this issue. For example, journalist John Judis and political scientist Ruy Texeira write "But one issue that concerned female voters directly as women and clearly turned many college-educated women toward the Democratic Party was the Republican Party's opposition to abortion." In support they cite women's opinions on the issue but nowhere compare them with those of men. See Judis and Texeira, *The Emerging Democratic Majority* (New York: Scribner, 2002): 54–55.

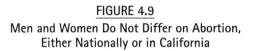

FIGURE 4.9

Men and Women Do Not Differ on Abortion,
Either Nationally or in California

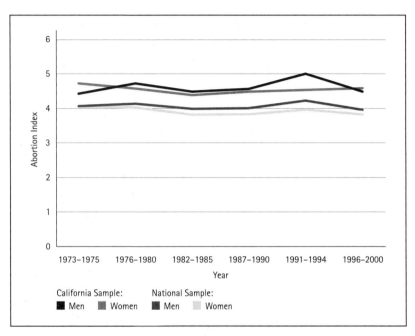

Source: Calculated from the General Social Surveys.

pro-choice than women—for understandable, if crass reasons. This negative finding extends beyond abortion to the full range of explicitly "women's issues." As Jane Mansbridge pointed out after the 1980 elections, men and women do not differ on such issues—contrary to widespread (mis)interpretations in the media and in the political arena, the roots of the gender gap lie elsewhere.[18]

18 Jane Mansbridge, "The ERA and the 1980 Elections," *Public Opinion Quarterly*, 49 (1985): 164–78. See also Elizabeth Adell Cook and Clyde Wilcox, "Feminism and the Gender Gap—A Second Look," *Journal of Politics* 53 (1991): 1111–1122.

Again, to emphasize that this lack of gender differences transcends the particular survey items used to examine them, we note that on the aforementioned Gallup survey item women are five to eight points more likely to favor legal abortion "under all circumstances" than are men, and also a couple of percentage points more likely to think that abortion should be "illegal in all circumstances" than are men. Figure 4.10 illustrates the minimal gender differences on this item.

Of course, one might object that even if men and women do not differ much on abortion, if women considered the issue much more important than men, a gap could still result. While this is an eminently plausible hypothesis that is accepted uncritically by many in the media and in politics, research finds little support for it. For example, in 1992 "feminist issues" (including abortion) were more important predictors of women's presidential votes than men's, but in 1996 the reverse was the case.[19] And a study of the gender gap in presidential voting between 1980 and 1992 concluded that abortion did not matter for either men or women in 1980, it mattered more for *men* in 1984 and 1988, and mattered for both men and women in 1992, although somewhat more for women.[20]

If the gender gap is not caused by abortion, then from what issues does it arise? Research finds that men's and women's views differ on two clusters of issues, a sampling of which appears in Table 4.4.[21] The first consists of issues of violence, the use of force,

[19] Karen Kaufmann and John Petrocik, "The Changing Politics of American Men: Understanding the Sources of the Gender Gap," *American Journal of Political Science* 43 (1999): 880–81.

[20] Carole Chaney, R. Michael Alvarez, and Jonathan Nagler, "Explaining the Gender Gap in U.S. Presidential Elections, 1980–1992, *Political Research Quarterly*, 51 (1988): 311–39.

[21] Robert Shapiro and Harpreet Mahajan, "Gender Differences in Policy Preferences: A Summary of Trends from the 1960s to the 1980s," *Public Opinion Quarterly* 50 (1986): 42–61.

FIGURE 4.10
When Should Abortion Be Legal? Men and Women Are Not Very Different

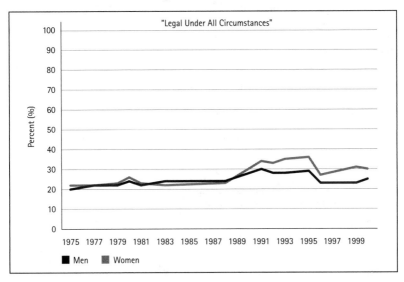

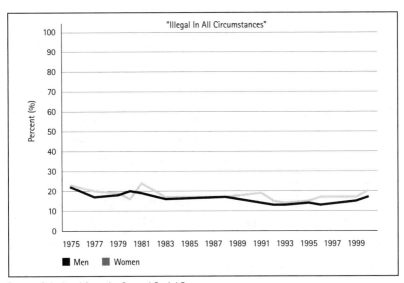

Source: Calculated from the General Social Surveys.

TABLE 4.4
Women's and Men's Attitudes Differ

	WOMEN	MEN
Role of Government		
Consider self conservative	29%	43%
Government should provide fewer services	30	45
Poverty and homelessness are among the country's most important problems	63	44
Favor affirmative action programs for blacks and other minority groups	69	58
Force/Violence		
American bombers should attack all military targets in Iraq, including those in heavily populated areas	37	61
Handguns should be illegal except for use by police and other authorized persons	48	28
Favor death penalty	76	82
Approve of caning the teenager in Singapore who committed acts of vandalism	39	61
Approve of the way the Justice Department took Elian Gonzalez from his Miami relatives	35	52

Source: *The Public Perspective*, August/September 1996: 10–27; *The Public Perspective*, July/August 1994: 96. Gallup Tuesday Briefing, May 2, 2000.

and peace and war. For example, women are less likely to support the death penalty, more likely to favor gun control, and less likely to favor going to war. A particularly striking example of this sort of gender gap emerged in 1994, when an American teenager living in Singapore who had vandalized property, was sentenced to a traditional Singaporean punishment of caning. A majority of the mothers and sisters of America considered the sentence barbaric, while a majority of the fathers and brothers viewed it as appropriate—the item produced a twenty-two-point gender gap.

The second cluster of issues on which men and women differ has to do with protecting the vulnerable—the aged, the sick, the poor, and other "at risk" categories. Women are more compassionate, registering higher levels of support for government programs to help the disadvantaged and greater willingness to support government spending for the disadvantaged.[22] Thus, women favor a more activist government than men, and are slightly more likely to label themselves liberals and less likely to label themselves conservatives.

Why do men and women differ in these ways? This is a matter of spirited debate. Some argue that gender differences are biological, that women and men are hard-wired differently. Others vehemently reject such arguments and attribute gender differences to cultural factors—women and men still are socialized to have different values. Still others contend that gender differences reflect the relatively greater economic vulnerability of women. The gender gap is much larger among single men and women than among married men and women.[23] So, as marriage rates have declined in recent decades the gender gap has grown accordingly.[24] Finally, some argue that the gender gap arises from different experiences and information. Even today women are far more likely to visit the aged and the sick in hospitals, volunteer in the schools, and otherwise see government programs in operation, while men think

---

[22] See, for example, Ann Beutal and Margaret Marini," Gender and Values," *American Sociological Review* 60 (1995): 436–48.

[23] See page 16 of the Pew Report discussed in the preceding chapter. A recent story in *USA Today* claims that married couples—especially educated ones—are increasingly split, but only anecdotes are presented in support. All the systematic data presented refer to men and women without regard to marital status. Susan Page, "Highly Educated Couples Often Split on Candidates," *USA Today*, December 18, 2003: 1A–2A.

[24] Lena Edlund and Rohini Pande, "Why Have Women Become Left-Wing? The Political Gender Gap and the Decline in Marriage," *Quarterly Journal of Economics* 117 (2002): 917–61.

of government mostly in terms of deductions from their pay-checks. Similarly, popular women's magazines and television programs focus on threats to the food supply and the environment and the necessity for mothers to protect their children, while popular men's magazines and television programs focus on women and sports. In contrast to men, women more often see the benefits of government programs as well as the costs.

As political scientists we are not professionally qualified to judge among such contending explanations of the gender gap. We can only emphasize that the gender gap in voting has its roots in gender differences on issues other than abortion. The reason that the gender gap has emerged in the past two decades is that the Democratic Party has come to be associated both with an activist government that supports the vulnerable and disadvantaged, and with a more pacifistic foreign and defense policy. In the mid-twentieth century, however, the Republican Party was seen as the party best able to keep the peace. In the 1950s, women voted for Republican Dwight Eisenhower at higher levels than men did. Eisenhower promised to end the war in Korea—and did—and declined to become involved in Vietnam. And as shown in Figure 4.8, women in 1960 voted more heavily for Eisenhower's vice president, Richard Nixon, than men did. After all, it was John Kennedy who was something of a saber-rattler in comparison, charging that the Eisenhower Administration had allowed a missile gap between the U.S. and USSR to develop, and taking a harder line on defending obscure islands off the coast of China.

Thus, in the mid-century decades women's differential preference for Republicans on the violence and war dimension roughly offset their preference for Democrats on the active government dimension. The emergence of an antiwar wing of the Democratic Party in the aftermath of U.S. involvement in Vietnam, however, changed the party's image. The Democrats came to be seen both as the more dovish of the two parties and the party more supportive of the welfare state, while the Republicans became the party with the more aggressive foreign and defense policy and the party hostile to the welfare state. As a consequence, differential gender preferences in the two clusters of issues now cumulate rather than offset as they did a generation ago.[25]

Although the preceding discussion of the gender gap might seem like something of a digression, it is quite relevant to the main line of our discussion. Commentaries on the culture war point to the gender gap as evidence that it exists: women supposedly are offended by the "orthodox" position on morality and sexuality; consequently, their support for the "orthodox" (Republican) party has declined. But if the gender gap arises from traditional issues of peace and war and social welfare, and not from the issue of abortion in particular, or issues of morality or sexuality more broadly, then that is further evidence that talk of a culture war is a misconception.

Given such evidence how did the belief that abortion underlies the gender gap become so widespread? The explanation probably lies in Groucho Marx' quip "who are you going to believe—me or your own eyes?" Feminist groups—almost by definition led by women— have taken the lead in supporting abortion rights, while

---

[25] This realignment of party images gave rise to Chris Matthews' famous characterization of the Democrats as the "mommy" party and the Republicans as the "daddy" party. For a more recent discussion see Jay Nordlinger, "Political Virility," *Wall Street Journal*, September 17, 2003: http://www.opinionjournal.com/extra/?id=110003887.

evangelical groups—usually headed by men—have taken the lead in opposing abortion rights. Politicians, activists and members of the media talk mostly to each other, so they make the natural but false assumption that the gender divide they see so clearly at the leadership level reflects a similar divide at the mass level.

Finally, it is also worth noting that the gender gap is not the result of women moving to the Democratic Party. That is another commonly believed myth. Rather, as a number of academic studies have noted, the gender gap primarily reflects the movement of men.[26] Men have moved away from the Democratic Party to the Republican Party, while the movement among women has been much smaller, as shown in Figure 4.11.[27] If the two parties are indeed engaged in a culture war, then Figure 4.10 suggests that over the past several decades, on balance more Americans have deserted than enlisted in the conflict.

EPILOGUE

On November 5, 2003 President Bush signed a bill outlawing so-called partial birth abortion except when necessary to save the life of the mother. Almost immediately cultural warriors opened fire. NARAL Pro-Choice America announced an ad campaign

---

[26] See, for example, Daniel Wirls, "Reinterpreting the Gender Gap," *Public Opinion Quarterly* 50 (1986): 316–30; Barbara Norrander, "The Evolution of the Gender Gap," *Public Opinion Quarterly*, 63 (1999): 566–76; Kaufmann and Petrocik, "The Changing Politics of American Men: Understanding the Sources of the Gender Gap," *American Journal of Political Science* 43 (1999): 880–81.

[27] To be precise, if leaning independents are treated as partisans, women show little change in their party identification over the past four decades, while men have moved away from the Democrats. If, as in Figure 4.10, leaning independents are treated as independents (as recommended by Warren Miller, one of the originators of the concept of party identification), then women have moved away from the Democratic Party, but at a slower rate than men. Warren Miller, "Party Identification, Realignment, and Party Voting: Back to the Basics," *American Political Science Review* 85 (1991): 557–568.

FIGURE 4.11
Men Have Left the Democratic Party Faster than Women Have

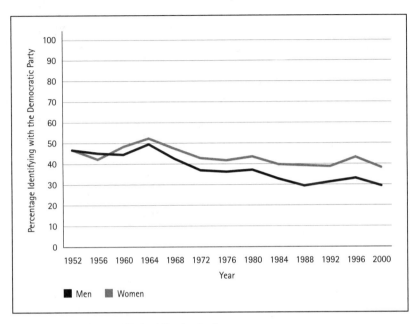

Source: Calculated from the National Election Studies.
Note: Partisans include strong and weak identifiers.

designed to meet the greatest threat to abortion rights in three decades. According to NARAL President Kate Michelman,

Together these spots serve as a stark reminder of what could happen if we don't stop this tidal wave of antichoice activity that is emanating right out of our own White House. The future health, safety and freedom of women in this country is in our hands. With antichoice leadership in Congress and the White House, and a razor-thin margin in the US Supreme

Court, pro-choice Americans must act today to protect their rights tomorrow.[28]

Meanwhile, Troy Newman of Operation Rescue contemptuously dismissed the significance of the legislation:

The new law signed by President G. W. Bush, similar to the bill twice vetoed by former President Bill Clinton, bans a narrowly defined act that is easily circumvented by the ever-crafty abortionist. It fallaciously includes a loop-hole exception to save the mother's life that many abortionists have routinely abused when included in other legislation.[29]

TV footage showed approving male representatives and senators watching President Bush sign the legislation, while disapproving women marched against the legislation, carrying signs and chanting slogans.

All of the myths about abortion and the culture war were on display here: extreme rhetoric, the contrasting genders of the pro-choice and pro-life spokespersons, and the contrasting genders of the legislative supporters and activist opponents. But beneath these images was the larger underlying reality that polls have consistently shown that two-thirds of the American citizenry opposes partial birth abortion except when the health of the mother is at stake. Reflecting that brute fact, majorities in both chambers of Congress—Democrats as well as Republicans voted for the bill. In prohibiting partial birth abortion except when the *life* of the mother is as stake, the bill actually went further than legislation

---

[28] http://www.oregonnaral.org/s04politicalupdates/press/200306201.shtml, accessed November 11, 2003.

[29] http://operationrescue.org/ftd/PBA_Ban2003Nov6.asp, accessed November 11, 2003.

that would have maximized popular support.[30] Perhaps for that reason, when the legislation was stayed by the courts, there was no great popular outcry against the decisions.

All in all, this particular episode confirms the general picture of abortion attitudes that we have described in this chapter: nuanced popular views of the issue reflected in majority approval of regulating some aspects of abortion, a gender gap among high-level political activists that is not apparent among ordinary Americans, and minimal partisan disagreement about the issue at the mass level contrasted with vitriolic conflict at the elite level.

---

[30] An *NBC News/Wall Street Journal* poll conducted immediately (November 8–10) after the bill signing found Americans far less supportive of the new legislation (47 percent in favor, 40 percent opposed, 13 percent not sure) than previous polls would have led one to expect. Here again we see the typical pattern: pro-choice forces supported a weaker alternative than the average voter would have preferred, while pro-life forces supported a more restrictive alternative.

CHAPTER 5

A Closer Look at Homosexuality

In June of 2003 the U.S. Supreme Court issued *Lawrence v. Texas*, striking down a Texas sodomy statute. The decision reversed *Bowers v. Hardwick*, a controversial 5-4 decision handed down in 1986. While legal scholars generally agree that *Lawrence* called into question all laws regulating private consensual sexual relations—heterosexual as well as homosexual, the decision was widely regarded as a victory for gay and lesbian activists for whom reversing *Bowers* had been a crusade. The *Lawrence* decision provoked a firestorm of criticism from those in the trenches of the culture war:

> *This is a major wake-up call. . . . This is a 9/11, major wake-up call that the enemy is at our doorsteps.*[1]

> *Has the end of the world arrived because the Supreme Court ruled no state may prohibit private, consensual homosexual*

---

[1] The Reverend Louis Sheldon, chairman of the Traditional Values Coalition at http://www.townhall.com/news/politics/200306/CUL20030627a.shtml, accessed September 4, 2003.

conduct? No, the end of the world is being handled by the Supreme Judge. But the end of the Constitution has arrived, and that is something about which everyone in this temporal world should be concerned.[2]

Issues of homosexual behavior and homosexual rights have not been prominent on the national agenda for as long as abortion, although gays and lesbians began to come out of the closet and organize politically in the early 1970s, about the same time that abortion rose on the political radar screen. Some conflicts erupted over local anti-discrimination statutes, but the issue largely simmered on the back burner until a backlash developed in the 1980s. The stinging rebuke Congress handed President Clinton in 1993 after he proposed allowing openly gay Americans to serve in the military seemingly demonstrated the intense views held by many ordinary Americans on this issue, and many believe that *Lawrence* has now made homosexuality and homosexual rights a second major front in the culture war.

Has it? After the decision there was no rioting in the streets, nor even much in the way of protests and demonstrations. To date there is little indication that anti-gay citizens are mobilizing to descend on Washington, as the pro-life forces have done. Instead, one poll reported that while almost a third of registered voters thought the Supreme Court's *Lawrence* decision "a disaster," a fifth said the decision was not important although they did not like it, another quarter said they did not really care, and the remaining fifth supported it.[3] True, gay marriage remains highly

2 Cal Thomas, "End of the Constitution?" http://www.townhall.com/columnists/calthomas/printct20030701.shtml, accessed September 4, 2003.
3 Poll reported by Andres McKenna Research, conducted July 8-10, 2003, http://nationaljournal.com/members/polltrack/2003/issues/03homosexuality.htm#3.

controversial, with a majority of Americans opposed. But the issue of gay marriage is only one element of the constellation of views Americans hold about homosexuality.

AMERICAN ATTITUDES TOWARD HOMOSEXUALS AND HOMOSEXUALITY

Describing Americans' attitudes toward homosexuality is difficult because unlike the other topics discussed in this book, public opinion in this area has been changing fairly rapidly, and in contrast to the case of abortion, broad movements in public opinion are significantly interrupted by reactions to current political events. We are attempting to describe a changing picture in this chapter, and it is far too early to come to any firm conclusions about a subject that may well change during the coming years.

To begin, there is no denying that Americans feel relatively cool toward gays and lesbians. For the past three decades the National Election Studies have included a measuring device called a "feeling thermometer," which asks people to assign a number that represents how warm or cold they feel about a group or person. The thermometer runs from zero to 100 degrees, and respondents are told that they should treat 50 as the neutral point. Almost all groups receive a net positive rating—even welfare recipients, anti-abortion activists, and "women's libbers" received an average rating a bit over 50 degrees in the years when those groups were included in the surveys. In 2000 Republicans were rated 54 and Democrats were rated 59.

Gays were unique in the 1980s in the number of people who gave them the coolest possible rating—zero, but as Figure 5.1

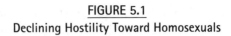

FIGURE 5.1
Declining Hostility Toward Homosexuals

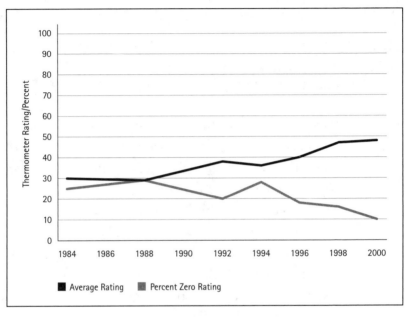

Source: Calculated from the National Election Studies.

shows that number has steadily declined, from almost a third in 1988 to less than 10 percent in 2000. Along with this sharp decline in extreme dislike, the average ratings of gays and lesbians have climbed significantly in the past fifteen years. In the 1980s gays and lesbians were rated at 30 degrees or colder, a level of dislike exceeded only by "black nationalists" in the 1970s. By 2000 however, gays and lesbians were rated only a few degrees on the cool side of the neutral point. By comparison, Christian fundamentalists, often viewed as the avowed political enemies of gays and lesbians, are rated just a few degrees on the warm side of the

FIGURE 5.2
What About Sexual Relations Between Two Adults of the Same Sex?

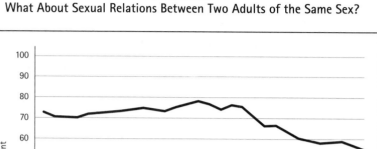

Source: Calculated from the General Social Surveys.

neutral point on the scale—about four degrees warmer in 2000. Blue state residents rated gays and lesbians at 51 degrees while red state residents rated them at 43 degrees, a difference more akin to a ditch than a chasm.

As is the case with abortion, majorities of Americans believe that homosexual relations are wrong. As shown in Figure 5.2, the General Social Surveys consistently find that a majority of Americans believes that sexual relations between two adults of the same sex is wrong, although the size of the majority that believes this has declined from more than three quarters to about 60 percent.

FIGURE 5.3

Should Homosexual Relations Between Consenting Adults Be Legal?

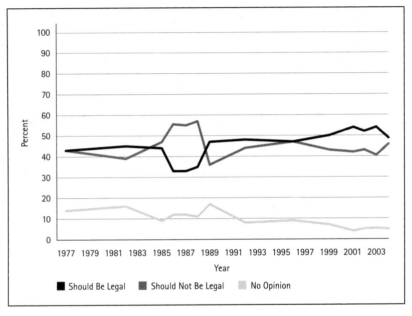

Source: The Gallup Organization.

But again as with abortion, a significant number of Americans who believe homosexuality is wrong decline to criminalize it.[4] Figure 5.3 shows a significant swing in opinion between the mid-1980s and today. Less than two decades ago solid majorities of Americans felt that homosexual relations should be illegal, but today a majority rejects that position.

Not only do Americans decline to criminalize behavior they believe to be immoral, they explicitly support protection of the

---

[4] For a detailed discussion see Jeni Loftus, "America's Liberalization in Attitudes toward Homosexuality, 1973–1998," *American Sociological Review* 66 (2001): 762–82.

FIGURE 5.4

Support for Equal Rights of Homosexuals in Employment
Has Steadily Increased

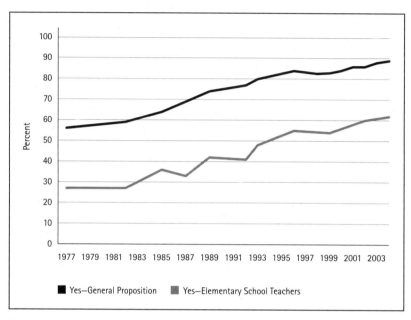

Source: The Gallup Organization.

rights of those they believe to be engaged in an immoral lifestyle.
Even in the mid-1980s when a majority of Americans felt that
homosexual relations should be illegal, majorities still supported
civil liberties for gays,[5] and Figure 5.4 shows that the percentage
of Americans who believe that gays and lesbians should have equal
job opportunities has grown steadily since the 1970s to the point
that there now is overwhelming support for equal employment

[5] In the 1984 and 1987 GSS surveys nearly 70 percent of respondents said that an admitted homosexual
should be allowed to speak in public, and only 40 percent favored removing a book advocating homosexuality from the library.

opportunities for homosexuals, including majority support for opportunities in occupations like teaching that as late as 1990 were considered too sensitive to permit the employment of homosexuals.

As with abortion, attitudes toward homosexuality differ across various categories of the population, but the differences are smaller than many might assume. Breakdowns of the Gallup data plotted in Figure 5.3 show that men and women differ little. Similarly, whites and nonwhites differ little. The expected regional dif-

FIGURE 5.5

Homosexual Relations Between Consenting Adults Should Be Legal: Expected Regional Differences Are Apparent

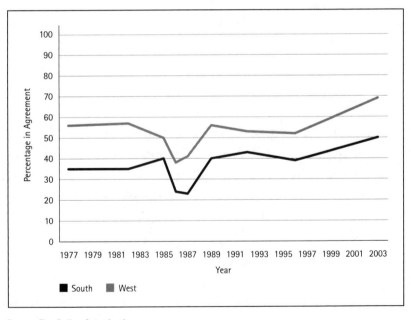

Source: The Gallup Organization.

ferences appear—there is about a 20 percent difference between the orthodox South and the libertarian West in the percent who would make homosexual relations legal, but even half the residents of the South now express that view (Figure 5.5). Gallup does not regularly subdivide Protestants into evangelical and mainline denominations, nor ask about church attendance, so we can not systematically compare denominational and religiosity differences, but a recent Gallup poll found that weekly churchgoers are only half as likely to favor legalization of homosexual relations as those who never attend church. But, again, 40 percent of weekly churchgoers favored legalization.[6]

THE AFTERMATH OF *LAWRENCE*

Despite the growing toleration of homosexual relations and the growing support for equal rights for homosexuals, at the present time a majority of Americans opposes gay marriage. We examined eleven poll items that asked about gay marriage in the aftermath of *Lawrence*.[7] Opposition ranged from 52 percent to 66 percent, with a median of 55 percent. Opposition to civil unions or domestic partnerships is slightly lower—fourteen polls reported a median opposition of 50 percent. Here is apparently an exception to the general pattern of earlier findings—a clear divide in public opinion, with a majority opposed to the recent direction of public policy in the area.

---

[6] Gallup poll, July 25–27, 2003.
[7] Some of these are contained in a very useful compilation of poll results by Karlyn Bowman, "Attitudes about Homosexuality" (Washington, DC: AEI Studies in Public Opinion, updated December 11, 2003). Others were found through an Internet search of various polling archives.

On the other hand, we did not find any noticeable backlash after the Supreme Court decision. A Gallup survey immediately after the decision reported a five-percentage-point *increase* in support for gay marriage, while another one in July reported a nine-point decrease in support for civil unions.[8] Pew found no change.[9] These are not the kinds of inconsistent figures one would expect if a deeply felt backlash were in progress. Moreover, although narrow majorities favor a constitutional amendment to ban gay marriages, by a 60:36 margin a majority of Americans opine that it is "not worth" amending the U.S. Constitution to outlaw homosexual marriage.[10]

Perhaps the politically most significant point to make about American attitudes toward homosexuality is the strong relationship such attitudes bear to age: younger Americans are more tolerant of homosexuals and more accepting of homosexual rights than older Americans. As Figure 5.6 suggests, although Americans of all ages are becoming more accepting, older cohorts that are dying off are being replaced by more tolerant younger cohorts. If commandants on the "orthodox" side intend to fight a culture war over homosexuality, they had better do it soon—their potential ranks are being thinned by mortality.

As we noted at the beginning of this chapter, at the time of this writing (December 2003) public opinion on homosexuality is moving as a reflection both of long-term trends and short-term political developments. Gay marriage may well be an important issue in the 2004 campaign which, in turn, might lead to changes

---

[8] Ibid., 19, 22.
[9] Ibid., 20.
[10] Ibid., 25–26.

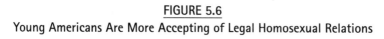

FIGURE 5.6

Young Americans Are More Accepting of Legal Homosexual Relations

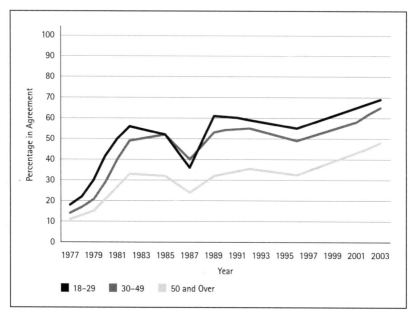

Source: The Gallup Organization. Note: Some data points have been aggregated from divergent age categories due to inconsistent measurement over time.

in the public's view of the issue. As of this writing both parties are treating the issue rather gingerly. The Democrats are naturally somewhat leery of the issue because of majority opposition to gay marriage, opposition that is strong among some of the party's traditional supporters.

Yet while many Republicans seemingly are responding to the wishes of the majority of Americans in supporting state and federal constitutional amendments to ban gay marriage, we think that the political benefits are smaller than might be assumed, and may even be negative. While most Americans are opposed to gay

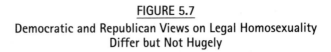

FIGURE 5.7

Democratic and Republican Views on Legal Homosexuality
Differ but Not Hugely

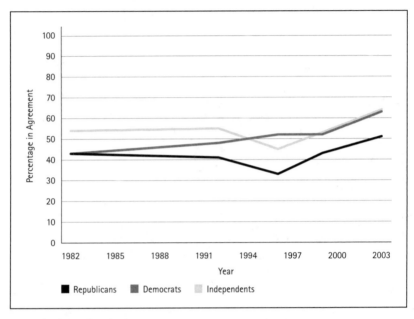

Source: The Gallup Organization.

marriage or even civil unions, we do not believe that many of them
have any wish for a vitriolic conflict over the issue. Certainly, the
recent history of antigay initiatives provides little evidence that
Americans are eager to endorse overtly antigay actions.[11] Moreover, given the direction in which opinion has been moving, and
the greater support for homosexual rights among young people,

---

11 "Of eleven statewide initiatives from the last two decades that are readily classifiable as antigay, only
three (27 percent) passed . . . When referenda written by a legislature are considered with initiatives, the
pass rate increases to 5 of 14 (38 percent) . . . Todd Donovan, Jim Wenzel, and Shaun Bowler, "Direct
Democracy and Gay Rights Initiatives After *Romer*," in Craig Rimmerman, Kenneth Wald, and Clyde
Wilcox, eds., *The Politics of Gay Rights* (Chicago: University of Chicago Press, 2000): 166.

any short-term political gains may well come with long-term costs if the Republicans become associated with antigay positions that are losing ground in the population.[12] At the present time Republicans and Democrats in the electorate differ on homosexuality, but as Figure 5.7 shows, even a bare majority of self-identified Republicans in 2003 favored legalization of homosexual relations, and independents—who hold the balance of electoral power— agree with Democrats on the issue.

As with abortion, there are obvious compromises that we think might attract the support of majorities of Americans—most obviously, the rights and duties of civil union without the name. Various European countries have been moving in this direction.[13] But we suspect that the views of activists on both sides of the issue will make it difficult for such compromises to get on the agenda. In frankness, however, there is not enough data to put such speculations on a firmer basis.

---

[12] Certainly President Bush's initial reaction to proposed constitutional amendments prohibiting gay marriage was more cautious than the sentiments of the Republican base would have led one to expect. Susan Page, "Bush's Gay-Marriage Tack Risks Clash with His Base," *USA Today*, December 18, 2003: 6A.

[13] Sarah Lyall, "In Europe, Lovers Now Propose: Marry Me, a Little," *New York Times*, February 15, 2004: 3.

CHAPTER 6

Have Electoral Cleavages Shifted?

The preceding chapters have reported numerous tables and charts inconsistent with the claim that Americans are deeply divided. Public opinion data fail to support a portrait of "two big separate voting blocks." On the contrary, there is little evidence that the country is polarized even on "hot button" issues like abortion. On the whole the views of the American citizenry look moderate, centrist, nuanced, ambivalent—choose your term—rather than extreme, polarized, unconditional, dogmatic. But why, then, does there seem to be a significant change in electoral cleavages in recent elections?

> *Whereas elections once pitted the party of the working class against the party of Wall Street, they now pit voters who believe in a fixed and universal morality against those who see moral issues, especially sexual ones, as elastic and subject to personal choice.*[1]

---

1 Thomas Edsall, "Blue Movie," *Atlantic*, January/February 2003: 36.

What demographic factor separates voters more than any other? The answer is—religion . . . the two Americas evident in the 48%-48% 2000 election are two nations of different faiths. One is observant, tradition-minded, moralistic. The other is unobservant, liberation-minded, relativist.[2]

Even if citizen attitudes on most issues are not highly polarized, has the way such attitudes translate into votes changed? That is, even if Americans are not deeply divided on specific issues, could it be that they translate their views into votes in new ways—ways that somehow magnify the differences that exist? Some differences may have declined in importance while others have greatly increased in importance, with the result that traditional cleavages like economics now are muted while others like morality now are amplified, producing voter alignments different from those of a generation ago. The notion of a culture war may be an exaggeration, but the common claim that politics is about religion and morality today more so than economics does not seem altogether inaccurate.

THE RISE OF RELIGIOUS CLEAVAGES

Various scholars have noted that presidential votes and party identification correlate more closely with religion today than a generation ago.[3] In this context "religion" does not refer to

---

[2] Michael Barone, *Almanac of American Politics* (Washington DC: National Journal, 2002): 27–28.
[3] The most recent and comprehensive work is Geoffrey Layman, *The Great Divide* (New York: Columbia, 2001).

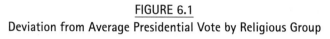

FIGURE 6.1

Deviation from Average Presidential Vote by Religious Group

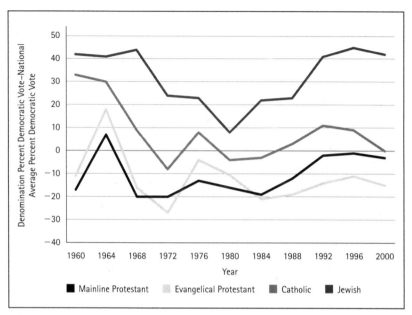

Source: National Election Studies.

denomination; rather, it refers to "commitment" or "religiosity." As shown in Figure 6.1, the relationship between presidential vote and denomination has eroded over the past generation or so. Catholics, in particular, are far less dependably Democratic today than they were prior to 1968, and mainline Protestants are less dependably Republican than they were in the 1970s and 1980s. Of particular note is the reversal of mainline and evangelical voting behavior in 1984. Prior to that election mainline Protestants were more Republican than evangelicals in every election save

1972—many southern Democrats at that time were white evangelicals, of course. After 1984 evangelicals are increasingly more Republican than mainline Protestants. Of the major denominations, only Jews are as supportive of a single party—the Democrats—as they were at mid-century, although there was a significant erosion of Jewish support for Democratic presidential candidates beginning in 1972 that was not fully erased until 1992.

If the relationship between partisanship and denomination has eroded, the same cannot be said for the relationship between partisanship and religiosity or religious commitment. On the contrary, in recent elections the more religious an individual, the more likely he or she is to vote for and identify as a Republican.[4] For example, Table 6.1 contrasts degrees of religious commitment within denominations. Protestants—both evangelical and mainline—who do not regularly attend church split much more evenly between Bush and Gore in 2000 than their fellow denomination members who regularly attend services. Among Catholics, electoral majorities actually reverse as regular churchgoers went for Bush by about the same margin as occasional churchgoers went for Gore.

Has religiosity become a significantly more important correlate of American voting behavior than it was in past decades? The available data indicate that the answer is yes. The longest available measure of religious commitment is one of church attendance, available since 1952 in the National Election Studies.[5] Since 1972

---

[4] Geoffrey Layman, "Religion and Political Behavior in the United States," *Public Opinion Quarterly* 61 (1997): 288–316.

[5] Religious commitment is a complex concept, to be sure, but church attendance is probably the most commonly used indicator. See the discussion in Karen Kaufmann, "What Men and Women Learn in Church: Religious Commitment and the Gender Gap in Party Identification," in press.

TABLE 6.1
Holding Denomination Constant, More Religious People Were More Republican in 2000

	BUSH	GORE
White Evangelical Protestants		
Regular attenders	84%	16%
Occasional attenders	55	45
White Mainline Protestants		
Regular attenders	66	34
Occasional attenders	57	43
White Roman Catholics		
Regular attenders	57	43
Occasional attenders	41	59

Source: John Green, James Guth, Lyman Kellstedt, and Corwin Smidt, "Faith in the Vote," *Public Perspective*, May/April 2001: 33–35.

respondents have been coded into five categories according to their frequency of attendance:[6]

1. Never
2. A few times a year
3. Once or twice a month
4. Almost every week
5. Every week or more

We have examined the relationship between church attendance and the Democratic presidential vote and find an increasingly strong association between church attendance and voting. In the

---

[6] There were NES question format changes in 1970 and 1990 that create some problems for comparisons over time. For a full discussion see the Appendix to this chapter.

1950s and 1960s the patterns are weak and variable—some categories are more or less Democratic, but they move around from election to election, and in some cases (1960) regular churchgoers are *more* Democratic. In 1972, however, a precursor of the contemporary relationship appears: Americans who never attended church were eighteen percentage points more likely to vote for McGovern than weekly churchgoers, perhaps a reflection of the "acid, amnesty, and abortion" charge levelled at the McGovernites. That relationship disappears in 1976 when a born-again Christian was the Democratic nominee, and remains weak and variable in the three 1980s elections. In 1992, however, a stronger version of the 1972 relationship appears and remains in 1996 and 2000. Figure 6.2 contrasts the voting behavior of the most and least religious Americans, showing that in the past three elections, those who rarely or never attend church have voted Democratic at a rate 20 to 25 points higher than the regular churchgoers.[7]

The stronger relationship between religiosity and voting that has developed recently appears to be genuine and not a spurious reflection of other factors. In Chapter 3 we described an earlier study of presidential voting aimed at explaining Al Gore's underperformance in 2000. That study analyzed presidential votes from 1972 to 2000 as a function of party identification, ideological self-classification, presidential performance evaluations, economic evaluations, and candidate evaluations. To those comprehensive equations we added variables representing the five categories of church attendance. The results confirm the preliminary conclusions

----

[7] We have combined the "never attend" and the "attend a few times a year" categories as the "nonattenders" and the "attend weekly" and "attend almost weekly" as the "attenders." For the rationale see this chapter's Appendix.

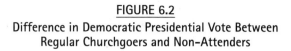

FIGURE 6.2

Difference in Democratic Presidential Vote Between
Regular Churchgoers and Non-Attenders

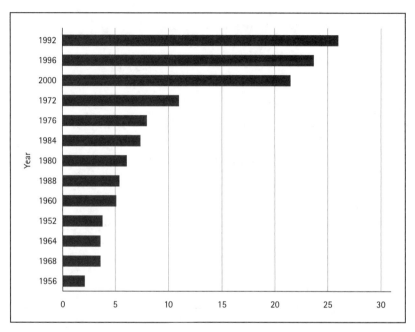

Source: National Election Studies.

from the figures. Over and above standard (and powerful) predictors of the vote such as party, ideology, presidential performance, and candidate evaluations, in the past three elections (but not before) church attendance has had a highly significant (statistically speaking) association with presidential voting.

Figure 6.3 plots the deviation of the Democratic vote in the more extreme church attendance categories from the Democratic vote in that election. This rearrangement of the data suggests two additional observations. First, as the figure graphically shows, the

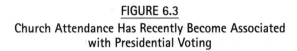

FIGURE 6.3

Church Attendance Has Recently Become Associated
with Presidential Voting

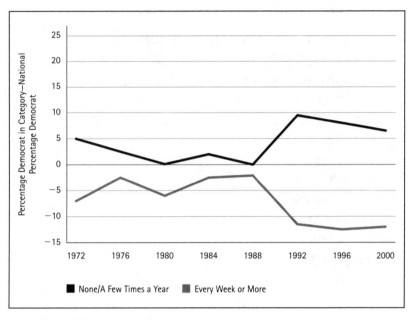

Source: National Election Studies.

contemporary association between religion and presidential voting did not develop gradually. Rather, it emerged suddenly and
dramatically in 1992. An explanation for that sudden emergence
will be offered in the next chapter. Second, although the resurgence of evangelical Christianity as a political force gets the lion's
share of the news coverage as well as scholarly attention, at least
in the realm of presidential voting, that resurgence is only part of
the story. As Figure 6.3 shows, the other important part is the
behavior of the unchurched. Their movement to the Democrats

since 1992 almost counterbalances the movement of weekly churchgoers to the Republicans, paralleling developments at the elite level,[8] and consistent with evidence that the movement of social conservatives to the Republicans has provoked a counter-movement of seculars to the Democrats.[9]

THE DECAY OF ECONOMIC CLEAVAGES?

So, religion in the sense of personal commitment has become a more important cleavage in recent American elections, consistent with the arguments of those who believe in the culture wars. But, do working class and Wall Street moralists now make common cause against blue-collar and Wall Street libertines, as Edsall suggests in the passage quoted earlier? Has the new cleavage of religion and morality eclipsed the old New Deal cleavage of class and income?[10] Far from it. Although religiosity has become more important, academic research indicates no decline in the importance of economics. On the contrary, comprehensive research indicates that income divisions are more important now than in earlier decades. In a 1997 monograph McCarty, Poole, and Rosenthal report that both party identification and presidential vote have become *more closely* linked to income since 1972.[11]

---

[8] Geoffrey Layman, "'Culture Wars' in the American Party System," *American Politics Quarterly* 27 (1999): 89–121.

[9] Louis Bolce and Gerald De Maio, "Religious Outlook, Culture War Politics, and Antipathy toward Christian Fundamentalists," *Public Opinion Quarterly* 63 (1999): 29–61.

[10] The religious cleavage is "new" only in a post-1928 view of American electoral history. The contemporary cleavage resembles the "Pietist-Liturgical" division that characterized much of American political history in the latter half of the nineteenth century. See, for example, Paul Kleppner, *The Third Electoral System, 1853–1892* (Chapel Hill: University of North Carolina Press, 1979).

[11] Nolan McCarty, Keith Poole, and Howard Rosenthal, *Income Redistribution and the Realignment of American Politics* (Washington, DC: AEI Press, 1997).

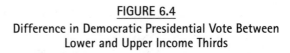

FIGURE 6.4
Difference in Democratic Presidential Vote Between Lower and Upper Income Thirds

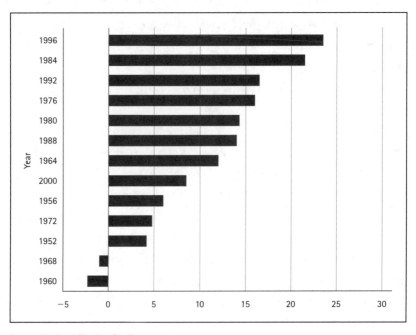

Source: National Election Studies.

And Stonecash and Lindstrom report that Congressional elections outcomes have become more closely related to district income in recent decades.[12]

Some simple data make the point clearly. In Figure 6.4 we plot the difference in the presidential vote (percent Democratic minus

---

[12] Jeffrey Stonecash and Nicole Lindstrom, "Emerging Party Cleavages in the House of Representatives, 1962–1996," *American Politics Quarterly* 27 (1999): 58–88. Stonecash and Lindstrom find that the relationship between district income and election outcomes has grown stronger in northeastern, mid-western, and southern congressional districts (about three-fourths of the total), but not in mountain and western districts.

percent Republican) between the highest and lowest thirds of the income distribution for the presidential elections since 1952. Evidently, income has been a far more important correlate of the vote in recent decades than it was several decades ago. The six elections that show the largest voting gap between low- and high-income voters occur between 1976 and 1996, while six of the seven elections with the smallest voting gap occur in 1972 or earlier, completely contradicting the claim that economics is a less important voting cleavage now than earlier. Interestingly, the one election that does not fit the contemporary pattern is 2000: the economic gap in 2000 was relatively small, more like that in 1964 than in the Reagan-Clinton elections. This could be the start of a trend, or it could simply be an aberration, but in light of the other years depicted in Figure 6.4, we think it would be highly premature to conclude that contemporary Americans consider economics less important than morality and religion.[13]

Moreover, note that in recent elections the difference in Democratic presidential vote percentage between the highest and lowest thirds of the income distribution is roughly comparable to the difference in Democratic vote percentage between the regular church attenders and those who do not attend services (compare Figure 6.2 and Figure 6.4). The glaring exception, of course, is 2000, where the religious difference is more than twice the economic difference, an occurrence that seems to have stimulated numerous claims that a new era has dawned in American politics.

---

[13] In opposition to the notion that religion has achieved a new status as the dominant political cleavage in the United States, one might cite the facts that (1) the economy was near the end of an exceptional run in 2000, and thus not an issue, and (2) national security concerns were minimal in 2000.

We do not wish to draw any firm conclusions about the relative importance of income and religious differences in contemporary elections. Such an estimate of relative importance would require a far more elaborate analysis than we have carried out, and analysts would argue at great length about the relative merits of measures and the most appropriate methods for analyzing the data. Suffice it to say that there is little evidence that economics has disappeared or even weakened relative to religiosity.[14] Claims about the demise of economic cleavages in American elections are true only if one limits one's focus to the drop-off from 1996 to 2000. Anyone whose time horizon is longer than the last presidential election can continue to believe that the divide between the working class and Wall Street is deeper today than it was at mid-century.

---

[14] Consider a simple statistical analysis that predicts presidential vote as a function of income and church attendance. Formally, we estimate a dummy variable logit model in which Vote = a + b_1 (highest income third) + b_2 (lowest income third) + b_3 (weekly church attendance) + b_4 (no church attendance). Considering the elections since 1972, when the relationship between religiosity and presidential vote first appeared, eight of the sixteen coefficients on the religious variables are significant, and eight of the sixteen coefficients on the income variables are significant. Neither of the income dummy variables is significant in 1972 or 2000. Neither of the religious variables is significant in 1988.

APPENDIX TO CHAPTER 6
Measuring Religiosity

We use the NES church attendance variable to construct a temporally comparable measure of religiosity. But although the variable appears in every NES survey between 1952 and 2000, using it requires dealing with three different question formats. The three versions of the item are as follows:

1952–1968

[If the respondent expressed a religious preference] Would you say you go to church regularly, often, seldom, or never?

- Regularly
- Often
- Seldom
- Never

1970–1988

[If the respondent expressed a religious preference] Do you go to church (synagogue) every week, almost every week, once or twice a month, a few times a year, or never?

- Every week
- Almost every week
- Once or twice a month
- A few times a year
- Never

1990–2000

Lots of things come up that keep people from attending religious services even if they want to. Thinking about your life these days, do you ever attend religious services, apart from occasional weddings, baptisms, or funerals? [If "Yes"]: Do you go to religious services every week, almost every week, once or twice a month, a few times a year, or never?

• Every week
• Almost every week
• Once or twice a month
• A few times a year
• Never

These changes in question wording are associated with shifts in the responses they elicit. For instance, in 1990 the addition of two qualifying phrases altered the cue given to respondents. Instead of simply asking people how often they attended services, the question began by noting that many things "keep people from attending" services. Probably even more important, the question ruled occasional attendance at weddings, baptisms, and funerals out of consideration. Figure A6.1 plots the trends for "a few times a year" and "never," and the effect of the 1990 question wording change is obvious. On the assumption that church attendance patterns are fairly consistent across time, or at least that they do not change abruptly from year to year, it appears that respondents who had previously answered "a few times a year," began to answer that they "never" attended services when confronted with the revised item. Thus, to create a temporally comparable measure

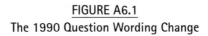

FIGURE A6.1

The 1990 Question Wording Change

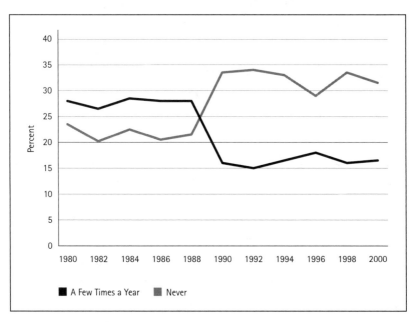

Source: National Election Studies.

from 1970 to the present we collapsed the two categories: "never" and "a few times a year" into a single category we label "nonattenders."

In 1970 not only did the question wording change, but the response categories did as well. Table A6.1 shows the distribution of church attendance across the four categories for 1968 and 1972. The far left-hand column shows the early question wording (1952–1968), and the far right-hand column shows the corresponding question wording for the later period (1970–1990). A comparison of the categories shows that they match up fairly

TABLE A6.1

Distribution of Church Attendance Reports by Pre– and Post–1970
Question Wording

EARLY QUESTION WORDING	1968	1972	LATER QUESTION WORDING
Never	12.1	16.5	Never
Seldom	34.6	29.6	A Few Times a Year
Often	15.4	15.7	Once or Twice a Month
Regularly	38.0	38.2	Every Week/Almost Every Week

Source: National Election Studies.

closely—particularly the categories "regularly" and "every week,"
and "often" and "once or twice a month."[1]

This gave us confidence that we could construct a time-series
that would accurately capture church attendance patterns over
time. Figure A6.2 plots our three-way categorization of church
attendance from 1952–2000. Church attenders are those who
reported going "regularly" from 1952–1968 and "every week" or
"almost every week" thereafter. Nonattenders are those who
reported no religious preference, "never," or "seldom" in the early
period and "never" or "a few times a year" in the later period. The
middle category consists of those who responded "often" in the
early period and "once or twice a month" in the later period. This
categorization produces a consistent time-series without sharp
spikes or breaks (as those seen above in Table A6.1), and we are

---

[1] The fact that the other categories do not match up as well is of less concern. Because of the 1990 question change those two categories are collapsed for our ultimate measure. Notice that when collapsing both categories the resulting measure is 46.7 percent not attending in 1968 and 46.1 percent not attending in 1972.

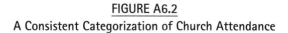

FIGURE A6.2
A Consistent Categorization of Church Attendance

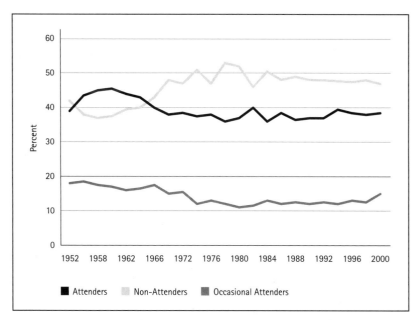

Source: National Election Studies.

therefore reasonably confident that this categorization of answers to the varying church attendance questions is the best available measure of religiosity for the period 1952 to 2000.

CHAPTER 7

Reconciling Micro and Macro

We have seen that the evidence for a culture war at the level of ordinary Americans is underwhelming. There is little indication that voters are polarized now or that they are becoming more polarized—even when we look specifically at issues such as abortion that supposedly are touchstone issues in the culture war. If anything, public opinion has grown more centrist on such issues and more tolerant of the divergent views, values, and behavior of other Americans. Despite the close results of recent national elections the country is not deeply divided. All of this data suggests that, for better or for worse, we are truly the "so-so nation."

But we have also seen that religion has become a more important electoral cleavage in recent years, although contrary to many claims by political commentators, so has economics. Moreover, political scientists have written numerous articles and books arguing that national politics is highly polarized, much more so than a generation ago.[1] The national parties are more distinct and more unified.[2] Congress is bitterly partisan. Presidents who received less than 50 percent of the popular vote nevertheless attempt to govern from the left (Clinton in 1993–1994) or right (Bush in 2002–2004) rather than from the center. Once-routine nominations to the federal courts have become occasions for ideological warfare.[3] And the op-ed pages and the political talk shows boil over with partisan and ideological vitriol. Moreover, contemporary "moral" or "values" issues like abortion and gay and lesbian rights were not even on the agenda a generation ago. Looking at the big picture, American politics indisputably has changed. How can we reconcile our view from the grass roots described in the preceding chapters with so many differing views from the treetops?

The key to understanding these inconsistent currents lies in the growing polarization of the political class—office holders, candidates, party activists, and interest group leaders. Their rhetoric, strategies, and behavior underlie the reality of national polarization, but it is elite polarization that is largely without foundation in a polarized electorate. Even if they still are centrists, voters can choose only among the candidates who appear on the ballot and vote only on the basis of the issues that are debated. Elites nominate candidates and set the agenda, and voters respond.[4] The idea

---

[1] See the essays in Jon Bond and Richard Fleisher, eds., *Polarized Politics: Congress and the President in a Partisan Era* (Washington, DC: CQ Press, 2000).
[2] Gary Jacobson, *The Politics of Congressional Elections*, 6th ed. (New York: Longman, 2004): ch. 8.
[3] Jennifer Dlouhy, "Senate Traditions a Casualty in Judicial Nominees Spat," *CQ Weekly*, July 12, 2003: 1735–37.
[4] One might object that on occasion a popular concern makes its way upward and elites are forced to respond. The tax revolt of the late 1970s is an example. Still, it is normally the case that one set of elites responds (the Republicans in the case of the tax revolt), forcing their opponents to do so as well. Note that both parties found it in their interest to downplay budget deficits during the late 1980s. Ross Perot's efforts forced the issue higher on the agenda.

that a culture war rages in the United States reflects observations of discourse and behavior within the political class. There, something that might be called a culture war does exist. And since the media are part of the political class and talk mostly to and about the political class, the misconception of popular polarization took root and grew.

CENTRIST VOTERS
AND POLARIZING ELITES

For as long as we have had data political scientists have known that political elites are more polarized than the mass of ordinary Americans. That is only natural—people who take the time and effort to participate in politics or hold office typically have strong feelings about issues. But in the past, electoral pressures constrained how much elites could indulge their own relatively more extreme preferences. In the 1950s, for example, a classic study reported that Democratic National Convention delegates were more liberal than Democratic party identifiers in the electorate and Republican National Convention delegates were more conservative than Republican identifiers in the electorate.[5] But the Republican delegates were further from their rank and file than the Democratic delegates were from theirs. Indeed, on a number of issues, the Democratic delegates were closer to the Republican identifiers than the Republican delegates were! This noteworthy disparity was widely interpreted as a good part of the explanation

---

[5] Herbert McCloskey, Paul Hoffman, and Rosemary O'Hara, "Issue Conflict and Consensus Among Party Leaders and Followers," *American Political Science Review* 54 (1960): 406–27.

for the Republican Party's minority status at mid-century. Given the political preferences of the era, only a candidate like Eisenhower—more moderate than the Republican activists who attended the conventions—could defeat a Democrat. In the old order when the parties followed their hearts rather than their heads, electoral disaster resulted—the Republicans in 1964 when American voters much preferred the echo to the choice,[6] and the Democrats eight years later when voters resoundingly demonstrated their willingness to whack either party when it strayed outside the mainstream.

Much has changed in the past half century, however. We will discuss these changes at greater length in the final chapter, but to sum up their cumulative impact, today's party activists and contributors are less likely to be motivated by material rewards than previously—tens of thousands of public employees no longer worry about losing their jobs if their party loses, and legal and programmatic changes have reduced the discretion of public officials to reward the individuals and groups who support them and punish those who oppose them. Moreover, a media ever alert for the scent of scandal watches carefully for material transgressions. Partly as a result of these developments, the old-time party machines with their associated corruption have largely disappeared.

What has replaced the old-time materially oriented party organizations are new-style organizations rooted in the advocacy groups that have exploded in number since 1960.[7] Intensely con-

---

[6] One of the Republican campaign slogans was "A Choice, Not an Echo."
[7] Kay Schlozman and John Tierney, *Organized Interests and American Democracy* (New York: Harper and Row, 1986); Jack Walker, *Mobilizing Interest Groups in America* (Ann Arbor, MI: University of Michigan Press, 1991).

cerned with issues, these organizations enroll members (or more often check-writers) who share their ideological and issue commitments. These groups and associations help provide the money and workers for today's campaigns and in all probability are generating more of the candidacies themselves.[8] The result is political activists and candidates whose ideological commitments run deeper than a generation ago, whose fear of losing elections is less than a generation ago, or both. For example, political observers estimate that almost three dozen of the fifty state-level Republican organizations are under the effective control of the religious right. In Chapter 3 we noted the polarization of party activists and strong partisans relative to the lower level of polarization among weak identifiers and independents in the electorate. Most observers believe that the polarization of the party bases and elected officials are intertwined.[9]

So long as only one party moves away from the center—like the Republicans in 1964 and the Democrats in 1972—electoral punishment results, and even ideologically motivated party activists eventually get the message, as did Democrat activists in the 1980s who got tired of losing and finally nominated a born-again southern governor who prayed at every opportunity, talked about the virtues of work and personal responsibility, allowed the execution of a mentally retarded prisoner to take place, and not incidentally, won the presidency. But if both parties move away from the center

---

[8] While theoretically plausible and supported by anecdotal evidence the latter is an exceedingly hard proposition to validate systematically, since data on the organizational and associational backgrounds of candidates must be compiled literally race by race.

[9] For example, Jacobson, *Politics of Congressional Elections*, 248–54; Richard Fleisher and Jon Bond, "Evidence of Increasing Polarization among Ordinary Citizens," in Jeffrey Cohen, Richard Fleisher, and Paul Kantor, eds., *American Political Parties: Decline or Resurgence* (Washington, DC: CQ Press, 2001).

and locate at a more or less equal distance away from the main-stream, then electoral punishment need not result. Voters will be less enthusiastic about their choices and about election outcomes than previously, but given a choice between two extremes, they can only elect an extremist.

Before proceeding, we emphasize once again that we are by no means the first to argue that the culture war is an elite phenomenon.[10] But some further development using standard political science theoretical tools enables us to show more precisely how elites can make electoral politics look polarized even when voters are not.

VOTER RESPONSE TO ELITE POLARIZATION

Political scientists often analyze elections with the aid of spatial models. The spatial metaphor is a staple of popular political commentary: candidates run to the right, move to the center, out-flank a competitor on the left, and so forth. Spatial models are formalizations of this common metaphor. The simplest model has candidates and voters arrayed along a single dimension, as illustrated in Figure 7.1. The dimension often is interpreted as left-right in the traditional economic sense—level of income redistribution, degree of government control of the economy, and other economic interpretations of economic liberal-conservative ideology. But a dimension can represent any type of issue—more or less

---

[10] That suggestion is contained in a number of the essays in Rhys Williams, ed., *Cultural Wars in American Politics* (New York: Aldine de Gruyter, 1997). See also E. J. Dionne, Jr., *Why Americans Hate Politics* (New York: Simon & Schuster, 1991).

FIGURE 7.1
The One-Dimensional Spatial Model

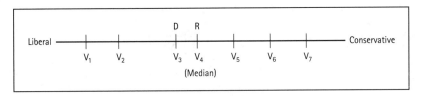

strict gun controls, more or less restrictive abortion laws, and so forth. Voters are distributed across the dimension with each one located at his or her "ideal point," a position where their happiness with government policy would be at a maximum. Voters are assumed to like a position less the greater its distance from them. Elections are decided by the positions of the candidates; in a two-candidate contest the candidate closer to a majority of voters wins.

Thus, in Figure 7.1 a Republican who locates at the median of the voter distribution (v_4) will defeat a Democrat who locates to his left at v_3 because the former will get the votes of the median voter (v_4) and everyone to his right (a majority by definition of the median). It can be shown quite formally that with everyone voting, the median is the equilibrium outcome—if two candidates locate at the median, neither can get more votes by moving.[11] This simple model provides the theoretical basis for the (formerly) widely held belief in the centrist tendencies of two-party politics.[12]

11 Duncan Black, *The Theory of Committees and Elections* (London: Cambridge University Press, 1958).
12 Anthony Downs, *An Economic Theory of Democracy* (New York: Wiley, 1957).

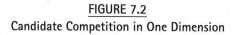

FIGURE 7.2
Candidate Competition in One Dimension

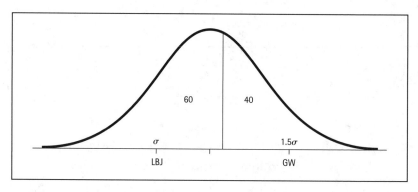

To begin our development, consider an idealized version of the 1964 election, as depicted in Figure 7.2. The electorate is normally distributed (that is, bell-shaped) on the economic dimension. Lyndon Johnson is a typical national Democrat who locates somewhat to the left of center (here pictured as one standard deviation from the center) on a dimension representing government intervention in the economy. In contrast, Barry Goldwater is a conservative Republican who wishes to give the voters a choice, not an echo. He locates farther away from the center on the right (pictured as one and one-half standard deviations in the figure). The result is that Johnson wins in a landslide with 60 percent of the vote (all those closer to him than to Goldwater, which is about 60 percent with the assumed normal distribution).

But suppose that even when Democrats were winning elections on economic policy there were a second dimension—a moral dimension—that no one noticed because the candidates did not differ on that dimension.[13] That is, voters always have had preferences concerning the moral beliefs and behavior of candidates, but those preferences never came into play forty years ago because candidates projected identical images. All (male) candidates had supportive, loving wives and nice, well-behaved children, went to church on Sundays, and in other ways paid homage to the ideal of middle-class morality. Consider that after Nelson Rockefeller divorced in 1962 many Republicans felt that he was no longer a viable candidate. When he remarried a divorcee (with children no less!) in 1963 the pre- and post-remarriage Gallup polls showed a 22 percent swing against him among Republicans.[14] The range of acceptable personal behavior was much narrower at mid-century.

Moreover, even if politicians then were secretly more "progressive" on the moral dimension, the media did not expose their transgressions, as revisionist accounts of the Kennedy presidency clearly show. The media at mid-century adhered to a different set of journalistic norms and a different concept of what was newsworthy, a concept that did not include adultery, affairs, drinking, drugs, groping, homosexuality, and other departures from conventional morality.

If voters have preferences concerning both the candidates' economic policies and their moral character and values, we need a two-dimensional representation, as depicted in Figure 7.3. The dynamics of this situation are best illustrated by passing a series of parallel planes through the distribution and focusing on the

---

13 Of course, there are still other dimensions such as race. The argument in the text would apply no matter how many "visible" dimensions there are. We posit only one visible dimension to keep the exposition simple.
14 John Kessel, *The Goldwater Coalition* (New York: Bobbs-Merrill, 1968): 44–45.

FIGURE 7.3
Candidate Competition in Two Dimensions

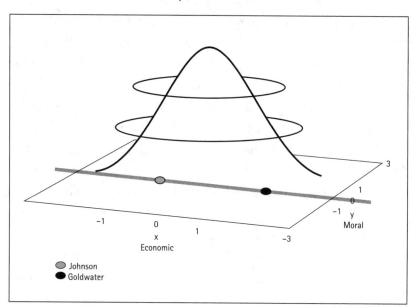

contours they generate, as in Figure 7.4. Analogous to a topographical map, these contours show the relative distance of voters from the candidates.[15] If we connect the Democrat and Republican positions with a line, the perpendicular bisector of that line separates the space into voters who are closer to the Democrat (west of the line) and voters who are closer to the Republican (east of the line).

Now assume that while the voters remain in the exact same position in the space, the candidates separate on the moral dimen-

---

[15] For convenience we assume that voters weight the two dimensions equally, which implies that voters prefer the candidate who is closer to them.

FIGURE 7.4
Candidate Competition in Two Dimensions: Aerial View

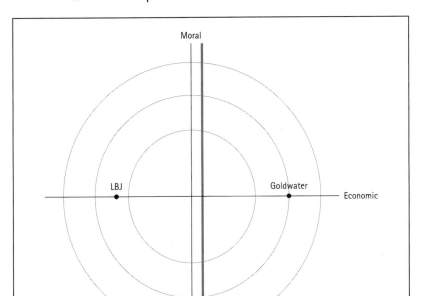

sion—Republicans move upward in a more "orthodox" direction and Democrats downward in a more "progressive" direction, with the Democratic candidate closer to the center of the electorate on the economic dimension, and the Republican candidate closer on the moral dimension.[16] We have drawn Figure 7.5 so that the Republican edge on the moral dimension exactly offsets the

---

[16] That is, during the Clinton years, public opinion generally favored the Democrat on economic issues but strongly disapproved of Clinton's personal behavior. While Clinton is no longer so prominent on the national scene, the association of the Democrats with nontraditional moral views remains.

FIGURE 7.5
Democrats and Republicans Separate on the Moral Dimension

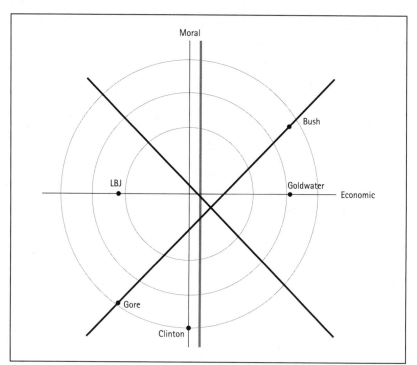

Democratic edge on the economic dimension—the two candidates are equidistant from the center, but one is closer on economics and the other on morality. In this case the election ends in a tie, roughly what happened in 2000.

Now compare Figures 7.4 and 7.5. By assumption, the voters have not changed: they hold exactly the same positions on the two dimensions and they follow the same behavioral rule—vote for the closer of the two candidates. But notice that the relationship between voters' economic positions and their votes changes between the figures. The cutting line that separates Republican from Democratic voters rotates to a northwest-southeast orientation: the candidates' electoral coalitions become more heterogeneous on the economic dimension. Bush now gets some support in the northwest from voters who are on the left of the economic dimension, while Gore now gets some support in the southeast from voters who are on the right of the economic dimension—some working class prudes are voting Republican while some Wall Street libertines are voting Democratic. Observing such voters, a casual observer might naturally conclude that economics matters less to voters in Figure 7.5 than in Figure 7.4. And observing that some variable, say, religious commitment, correlates with position on the moral dimension, a casual observer might further conclude that religion now matters more to voters.

These are the wrong conclusions, however justified they seem. By assumption voter positions have not changed, nor has their behavior: each voter supports the candidate closer to his or her (unchanged) position. The observed change in the candidates' support simply reflects the fact that the candidates have separated on the moral dimension. To make this point a little more rigorously, we have carried out a series of computer simulations, as outlined in Figure 7.6. In each simulation voter positions are the same,[17] and the voter decision rule is the same: vote for the closer of the two candidates. But in three steps we change the candidates' positions from those depicted in Figure 7.4 to those depicted in Figure 7.5: the two candidates gradually move apart on the moral dimension until their positions exactly offset their respective positions on

---

[17] Each simulation uses an identical bivariate normal distribution of voters.

FIGURE 7.6
Simulation: Unchanging Voters, Moving Candidates

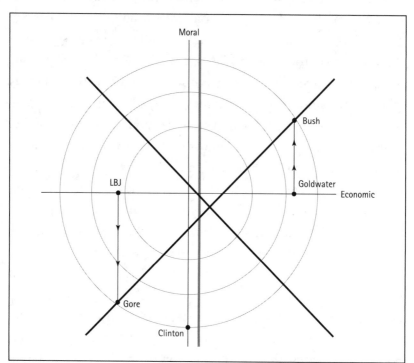

the economic dimension. At each of the four stages we carry out a standard political science statistical analysis that relates the voter's presidential choice to his or her positions on the economic and moral dimensions. Figure 7.7 plots the estimated coefficients.[18]

Any analyst looking at Figure 7.7 would view it as persuasive evidence that over the course of the four election series the deter-

---

[18] These are logit estimates for the equation Vote = a_1 + b_1 (voter economic position) + b_2 (voter moral position). Coefficients are negative because the farther the candidate is from the voter's position, the less likely the voter is to support that candidate.

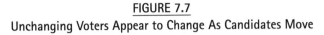

FIGURE 7.7

Unchanging Voters Appear to Change As Candidates Move

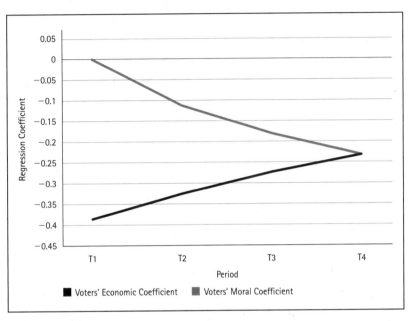

minants of the presidential vote have changed significantly: economic position has weakened and moral position has strength-
ened to the point that both are of equal importance. In a sense,
this is true: the correlates of the vote have changed. But this is not
because voters have polarized on the moral dimension, nor that
they have increased the weight they attach to that dimension (or
decreased the weight they attach to the economic dimension)—by
assumption voters have not changed. Rather, unmeasured changes
in the positions of the candidates make it appear that voters have
changed. The point has extremely important (and damaging)
implications for literally hundreds of electoral analyses carried out

over the past forty years. Because candidate positions generally are not measured (how does Dwight Eisenhower compare to Robert Dole? Adlai Stevenson to Bill Clinton?), even when studies use identical measures of voter attitudes, statistical estimates will confound voter change with candidate change.[19]

To return to the real world, we can now put discussions of the culture war in perspective. When candidates diverge (converge) on an issue dimension, voters will appear to weight that dimension more (less) heavily even if their own preferences and decision rules do not change. Thus, when the Republicans nominated economic conservatives such as Ronald Reagan and George Bush Sr., and the Democrats nominated mainstream economic liberals like Jimmy Carter and Walter Mondale, all of whom stayed pretty close to the center on the moral dimension, we did not hear much about culture wars.[20] But the Republicans moved closer to the religious right, and then Bill Clinton arrived on the scene. With Bill Clinton the electorate got an admitted adulterer, a confessed marijuana smoker (but not inhaler), and a champion of gay rights. These were pretty clear signals that he was located on the "progressive" side of the moral dimension.[21] In our view the dramatic rise in the relationship between religiosity and the vote depicted in Figure 6.3 of the preceding chapter probably reflects the emergence of Bill Clinton in presidential politics, rather than a sudden

---

[19] See the Appendix to this chapter for a more detailed explanation.

[20] Recall that activists in the religious right complained that Reagan paid only lip service to their issues.

[21] Additionally, Clinton moved the Democratic Party closer to the center on economic issues. Kaufmann is one of the few analysts who have recognized the consequence of such candidate movements when she argues, "As much as any other factor, I believe that the right turn of the Democratic Party on fiscal issues is responsible for the notable salience of cultural issues in the 1990s." Karen Kaufmann, "Culture Wars, Secular Realignment and the Gender Gap in Party Identification," *Political Behavior* 24 (2002): 283–307.

increase in the political importance of religion to voters. The 1972 foreshadowing of the stronger relationship is consistent with this hypothesis: the McGovern campaign was associated with what was then called the "counterculture" with its purported rampant drug use and its rejection of traditional sexual mores.

Note that the preceding discussion undermines not only any conclusions about the changing relationship between religiosity and vote, but also analogous conclusions about relationships between religiosity and party identification. Simply substitute Democratic and Republican Parties for Democratic and Republican candidates, and the same conclusion holds. Thus, the common observation that religiosity now is more closely related to party identification may reflect a repositioning of the parties rather than a change in voter attitudes. The Republican Party has become closely allied with white evangelicals, while the Democratic Party has become more assertively secular. Any attempt to compare the correlations between voter positions and political evaluations over time runs the risk of attributing changes in the correlations to changes in voter attitudes when it may be that the positions of the objects of political evaluation—candidates, parties, and groups—have changed.[22]

Before concluding this discussion we emphasize a number of caveats to our discussion. First, we are not claiming as a matter of fact that voters have not changed at all since the 1960s. A generation has passed from the scene and another has been born, not to

[22] For example, Pew reports that religiosity has become more closely associated with liberal-conservative self-identification. However, if liberal and conservative once were largely economic in their meaning but now have taken on moral or cultural issue connotations, then the argument in the text applies to this claim as well.

mention that continuing members of the electorate change their minds as they age and undergo different life experiences. But our argument does show that it is difficult in practice to separate voter change from candidate and party change, and that it is all too easy to mistake the latter for the former. We suspect that such mistakes explain the existence of myths like the culture war. Elites have polarized, but the public opinion data reviewed in chapters 2–5 provide little reason to believe that elites are following voters. Rather, they are imposing their own agendas on the electorate.

Second, we are not asserting that voter perceptions necessarily are accurate. Aggrieved Democrats may protest our characterizations of President Clinton as a violator of conventional morality and George W. Bush as an upholder of conventional morality, citing Bush's past alcohol abuse and rumors of cocaine use and extramarital affairs. The reality is not at issue, however; voter perceptions are. And on that score, our depictions are accurate. Despite Clinton's generally high job approval ratings, his personal ratings were always significantly lower and dropped further during his scandal-ridden administration.[23] And a new item on the 2000 National Election Study survey asked respondents whether since 1992 the country's moral climate had gotten better, worse, or stayed the same. Only 5 percent said it had gotten better, and 45 percent said it had gotten worse.

All in all, it may well be that the myth of a culture war, misconceptions about voter polarization, and mistaken claims about the rising importance of religion vis-à-vis the declining importance of

---

[23] "As the Scandals Have Persisted, Clinton's Standing on Matters of Integrity Has Plunged," *The Public Perspective*, October/November 1998: 24–35.

economics all have their roots in the arrival of Bill Clinton on the national scene. The obvious counterfactual would be to observe the voting behavior of the American electorate if the Democrats were to nominate a candidate who strongly upholds traditional morality (in actuality, not just in rhetoric).[24] In that event the implication of this analysis would be that the relationship between voter religiosity and candidate choice would be muted.

---

[24] Senator Joseph Lieberman probably would be the closest example.

APPENDIX TO CHAPTER 7

A Deep Identification Problem in Electoral Studies[1]

During the course of this research we came to the realization that the findings of scores if not hundreds of electoral studies are ambiguous. The problem most deeply afflicts attempts to study electoral change by conducting successive cross-sectional analyses and comparing the results.[2] Typically researchers assume that so long as survey measures are temporally comparable, statistical estimates based on the survey data will be comparable as well. As the examples in Chapter 7 show, however, that is not generally the case.

Consider that in the short span of eight years the popular vote for president in the latter half of the twentieth century varies from more than 60 percent Democratic (1964) to more than 60 percent Republican (1972). How can this variation be explained? The standard way to proceed is to identify a set of predictive variables that are available for all the elections to be analyzed. Such variables would include voters' partisan self-classifications, their ideological self-locations, and their positions on various issues such as taxation, abortion, racial policies, defense policies, and others.

Often researchers distinguish between "distributional" change and "behavioral" change. The former refers to variation in the distribution of voter attitudes—from election to election there are fewer liberals, more Democrats, fewer opponents of racial policies, more opponents of abortion policies, and so on. Variations in

---

[1] We thank Michael Herron of Northwestern University for this title.
[2] Rather than point the finger at any of our guilty colleagues, we point to an example of the problem in Morris Fiorina, "The Electorate in the Voting Booth," in Michael Nelson, ed., *The Parties Respond.* (Boulder, CO: Westview Press, 1990): Table 6.4.

the number of people who fall into various categories normally will produce electoral change, even if there is no change in the importance people attach to issues or in the relevance of ideological and partisan classifications for voting.[3] Conversely, even if the number of people who fall into various categories does not change, electoral change might still occur because the relative importance of the issues and classifications changes. The latter, represented by different coefficients in statistical models, sometimes is referred to as behavioral change.

But there is a third kind of change that goes unrecognized in cross-sectional studies—changes between elections in the positions of the candidates. Changes in candidate positions are brought into the analysis as qualitative side information that provides a plausible account for any behavioral changes that are uncovered. For example, a number of scholars concluded that voters became more ideological and issue-oriented in the 1960s than in the 1950s (distributional and behavioral changes) in part because of the greater issue and ideological differences in the 1964 and 1968 campaigns.[4] The point we made in this chapter is more subtle than the argument that candidates can affect how voters behave. Our point is simply that candidate change can produce the *appearance* of voter change even in the absence of the latter.

It is relatively easy to determine if average voter positions are constant from election to election, so long as comparable measures of the independent variables are available from election to

---

[3] To be precise, this will be the case if the relative probabilities of voting for Democratic and Republican candidates differ among categories that gain and lose people and do not net out in the aggregate.
[4] See the symposium in the June 1972 *American Political Science Review*.

election.[5] And changes in the distribution of independent variables generally will not result in changes in the coefficients. Thus, distributional change can typically be identified and its effects parsed out.[6] The more serious problem is that in the absence of distributional change, temporal changes in the coefficients can reflect either behavioral change on the part of voters, as discussed above, or changes in the positions of the candidates—as shown in this chapter. If candidates converge (diverge) on an issue it will appear to have less (more) importance to voters even if voters have constant judgments of how important the issue is. Thus, a finding that race has declined as a correlate of voting may mean either that voters judge race to be a less important issue, or that the candidates are taking positions close to each other, or both.

This confounding of effects is not limited to issue variables that explicitly mention distance. Consider the classic party identification scale. Numerous scholars have attempted to analyze variation in the importance of partisanship across elections. But none of their analyses incorporate the partisanship of the candidates. That might seem a peculiar statement, given that in each election a Republican opposes a Democrat, but if both parties were to nominate moderate partisans (like a Dwight Eisenhower), one would expect party identification to be less predictive than if both were to nominate hard-core partisans (like a Bob Dole). If one nominates a moderate partisan and the other a hard-core partisan, still other variations in coefficients will result.

---

[5] There is always the question of whether a survey item asked in the context of 1976 means the same thing when asked in the context of 1996, but as a profession we rarely discuss that question.

[6] For a classic example, see Donald Stokes, "Some Dynamic Elements of Contests for the Presidency," *American Political Science Review* 60 (1966): 19–28.

The same is true for ideological self-classification. If both parties nominated middle-of-the-road candidates, one would expect ideological self-categorization to matter less than if a hard-left Democrat ran against a hard-right Republican. Numerous variables that on their face do not seem to be distance variables, on reflection have a distance component that is unmeasured in typical analyses.

So-called proximity measures do not solve the problem because changes in voter proximity to candidates from election to election can reflect changes in voter position, candidate position, or both. Our simulations (to be reported in a future paper) indicate that the coefficients on proximity measures vary with changes in candidate positions even when voter positions and voter decision rules stay constant. For example, a finding that relative closeness to the candidate on economic policy matters more than previously may indicate either that voters regard economic policy as more important or that the candidates have moved relatively farther apart, or both.

CHAPTER 8

How Did It Come to This and Where Do We Go from Here?

As its name suggests, political science is a discipline that encompasses both the political and the scientific. In the preceding chapters we have made every effort to practice the "science" part of the compound name—the chapters examine a number of factual claims about contemporary American politics, evaluate their accuracy, offer alternative interpretations of the data, and generally attempt to improve on existing descriptions of the state of our politics. This chapter falls somewhat more under the "political" part of political science. The arguments are broad, the evidence is unsystematic or impressionistic, and the discussion reflects the personal values and judgments of the author. For that reason I absolve my two able associates, Samuel Abrams and Jeremy Pope, from any responsibility for this chapter. Their good work contributed greatly to any merit the preceding chapters have, but they are not implicated in this chapter, which reflects the views of someone who has been studying, teaching, and writing about American politics for more than thirty years, someone whose affection for the subject has been diminished by its current condition. Much has changed in American politics since the middle of the twentieth century. Looking back, the interaction of three major developments now seems to me to be of great importance for the state of politics today.[1]

THE ASCENDANCE OF THE PURISTS

In 1962 James Q. Wilson published *The Amateur Democrat*, discussing the rise of the "amateurs" (a term he was not altogether satisfied with), and contrasting them with the "professionals" who had dominated American politics at least since the rise of mass parties in the 1830s.[2] A few years later, Aaron Wildavsky wrote about the "purists" who snatched the Republican Party away from the professionals in 1964 and nominated Barry Goldwater.[3] According to Wilson, the professional

. . . is preoccupied with the outcome of politics in terms of winning or losing. Politics, to him, consists of concrete questions and specific persons who must be dealt with in a manner that will "keep everybody happy" and thus minimize the pos-

---

[1] The discussion that follows draws on and extends the discussion in two of my earlier articles, "Extreme Voices: A Dark Side of Civic Engagement," in Theda Skocpol and Morris Fiorina, eds., *Civic Engagement in American Democracy* (Washington, DC: Brookings, 1999): 395–425; "Parties, Participation, and Representation in America: Old Theories Face New Realities," in Ira Katznelson and Helen Milner, eds., *Political Science: The State of the Discipline* (New York: Norton, 2002): 511–41.
[2] James Q. Wilson, *The Amateur Democrat* (Chicago: University of Chicago Press, 1962).
[3] Aaron Wildavsky, "The Goldwater Phenomenon: Purists, Politicians and the Two-Party System," *Review of Politics* 27 (1965): 386–413.

sibility of defeat at the next election. . . . Although he is not oblivious to the ends implied by political outcomes, he sees . . . the good of society as the by-product of efforts that are aimed, not at producing the good society, but at gaining power and place for one's self and one's party.[4]

Wildavsky's characterization of the professional is similar:

The belief in compromise and bargaining; the sense that public policy is made in small steps rather than big leaps; the concern with conciliating the opposition and broadening public appeal; and the willingness to bend a little to capture public support. . . .[5]

In contrast, Wilson's amateur

. . . is one who finds politics intrinsically interesting because it expresses a conception of the public interest. The amateur politician sees the political world more in terms of ideas and principles than in terms of persons. Politics is the determination of public policy, and public policy ought to be set deliberately rather than as the accidental by-product of a struggle for personal and party advantage.[6]

Similarly, the distinguishing characteristics of Wildavsky's "purists" are

. . . their emphasis on internal criteria for decision, on what they believe "deep down inside"; their rejection of compromise; their lack of orientation toward winning; their stress on

---

4 Wilson, *The Amateur Democrat*: 4.
5 Wildavsky, "The Goldwater Phenomenon": 396.
6 Wilson, *The Amateur Democrat*: 3.

*the style and purity of decision—integrity, consistency, adher-
ence to internal norms.*[7]

In these writings a generation ago Wilson and Wildavsky
identified the wave of the future. In contrast to the 1950s, we no
longer think of the Democrats as a cadre of political professionals
leading a broad coalition of blue-collar working people, and
Republicans as an opposing cadre leading a smaller but still broad
coalition of white collar professionals and managers. True,
unions, especially the public employee unions, continue to play an
important role in the Democratic Party, as business does in the
Republican, but today we are more likely to think of the Democrats as the party of the environmental, civil rights, pro-choice,
gay-lesbian, and gun control groups, and the Republicans as
the party of the pro-life, traditional values, antitax and pro-gun
groups. Issue activists—Wildavsky's purists—largely define the
party images today.

Why the change? As noted in the preceding chapter, to some
extent it reflects the decline of material incentives for political participation. The implications of party control of government for
employment opportunities greatly diminished as civil service protection and public sector unionization spread. Similarly, as men-
tioned in the preceding chapter, conflict of interest laws, government in the sunshine laws, ethics codes, and investigative media
made it harder to reward one's friends and punish one's enemies
than a generation ago. As material incentives declined, fewer
political activists were drawn from the ranks of people having a

---

[7] Wildavsky, "The Goldwater Phenomenon": 399.

personal material stake in political participation.[8] More and more the field was left to those with policy or ideological motivations. To the former, compromise was a means to achieving their (material) goals; to the latter, compromise directly devalues their (ideological and programmatic) goals.

The increased importance of money in modern campaigns also contributed to the ascendence of the purists. Understandably, poor people don't contribute.[9] In order to raise money the Democrats had to move upscale and cultivate middle-class issue activists who had money to give. Thus, the economic liberalism of the 1950s Democrats evolved into the lifestyle liberalism of the 1980s. For the Republicans money was in less short supply than voters, so the Republicans allied with religious-right groups as a way of attacking the Democrats' majority status. The strategy succeeded, but by the 1990s the activist tail had come to wag the party dog. The economic conservatism of the 1950s Republicans has evolved into a social conservatism that dismayed Barry Goldwater before his death.

Finally, the media has made its contribution to the rise of the purists. People with deep issue commitments who express them in loud chants and strident rhetoric provide good copy and footage. The smallest demonstration will attract a camera crew and give a spokesperson or two the opportunity to provide a colorful quotation or sound bite. Seeing the success of fellow purists in getting

---

[8] I emphasize the importance of the modifier "personal." Obviously the material consequences of government action are larger today than ever before. But whether you personally benefit from or suffer those consequences today has less to do with your political involvement than in the past. For example, in few cities today would a neighborhood lose its garbage collection for voting the "wrong way."
[9] Sidney Verba, Kay Schlozman, and Henry Brady, *Voice and Equality* (Cambridge, MA: Harvard, 1995): 361–66.

recognition by the media, others no doubt were encouraged to follow a similar path. In a 1995 study Jeffrey Barry analyzed all evening news programs on the three major networks plus CNN, and reported that citizens' groups, composed largely of what we call purists, received a disproportionate share of coverage: "Although they were but a small part of the lobbying population, citizen groups constituted 45.6 percent of all the interviews with interest group representatives, mentions of specific lobbying organizations, and references to interest group sectors."[10]

THE EXPANSION OF GOVERNMENT

A second major development of the past half century is the expansion of government into spheres of life previously considered to be private. In the 1950s the idea that an apartment manager or bank loan officer should not be permitted to discriminate against members of a racial or ethnic minority was a highly contested notion. The idea that a developer could not fill in a swamp because of the presence of a salamander would have seemed ludicrous, let alone the notion that a citizen could petition government for a smoke-free environment.

The literature associates the expanded scope of government with a broad confluence of factors. An increasingly enlightened population demanded that long-festering racial injustices be redressed. An increasingly affluent population turned its attention to quality-of-life issues like the environment. What Mary Anne

[10] Jeffrey Berry, "The Rise of Citizen Groups," in Theda Skocpol and Morris Fiorina, eds., *Civic Engagement in American Democracy* (Washington, DC: Brookings, 1999): 381.

Glendon called the "rights revolution" enabled citizens to petition the courts for broad remedies to correct newly defined injustices.[11] Whereas rights battles once revolved around such weighty matters as voting, housing, and employment, aggrieved citizens now assert rights to exercise their dogs in public spaces, to be free of cigarette smoke out of doors, and to breast-feed in public.[12] Once a feminist rallying cry, "the personal is the political" spread far beyond its original context to become a general call for consistency between one's private behavior and public principles. But that consistency could be achieved not only by changing one's private behavior, but also by demanding that the public sector enforce one's personal principles.

Thus, education, affluence, and ideology supported demands for a vast increase in the sphere in which government could operate. The net result of these and other developments was a huge expansion in the jurisdiction of the public sector—the "new social regulation" of the 1960s and 1970s.[13] On the local level Nancy Burns reports a near-tripling in the number of "special districts" (local jurisdictions that deal with environmental, conservation, recreation, and other specific subjects) between mid-century and 1987, from a bit more than ten thousand to about thirty thousand.[14] No one can count the expansion of government as measured in total number of restrictions, regulations, and permits, or in

---

[11] Mary Anne Glendon, *Rights Talk: The Impoverishment of Political Discourse* (New York: Free Press, 1991).

[12] I am not opposed to such demands; indeed, I am in favor of many of them, but elevating them to the level of rights exaggerates their importance as well as diminishes the importance of fundamental rights.

[13] William Lilly and James Miller, "The New Social Regulation," *Public Interest* 47 (1977): 49–62; David Vogel, "The 'New' Social Regulation in Historical and Comparative Perspective," in Thomas McGraw, ed., *Regulation in Perspective* (Cambridge, MA: Harvard University Press, 1981): 155–64.

[14] Nancy Burns, *The Formation of American Local Governments: Private Values in Public Institutions* (New York: Oxford University Press, 1994): 6.

the different areas of life in which government began to operate.

The expansion of the scope of government created myriad new opportunities for those with particular issue concerns to become active in politics. There have always been people who felt extraordinarily strongly about the height and color of neighbors' fences, the contents of children's textbooks, the serving of foie gras in restaurants, and so on, but in past times they were called cranks or busybodies and were generally ignored or left to settle their conflicts informally. Today they are called activists and they demand government action to enforce their views. A party that adopts the narrow agendas of such activists can enlist their energy and resources in support of its candidates.

THE RISE OF
PARTICIPATORY DEMOCRACY

At about the same time that ideological and issue motivations for political participation were on the rise, and the scope of government was expanding, the United States experienced a significant participatory turn. Consider Table 8.1, which lists some of the important changes in politics between the elections of John Kennedy and Bill Clinton.

The most widely recognized of these changes is the transformation of the presidential nominating process. John Kennedy was nominated by Democratic Party professionals—cigar-chomping "bosses" who met in smoke-filled rooms, according to the popular image. Only four years later Goldwater was nominated by Wildavsky's purists, and eight years after that, opposing purists captured the Democratic party and nominated George McGovern,

TABLE 8.1
Changes in American Politics Since 1960

Presidential nominating process

"Candidate-centered" politics

Open meetings

Recorded votes

Expanded rules of standing

Enhanced judicial review

Open bureaucracy

Intervenors

"Maximum feasible participation"

Proliferation of local bodies

Advocacy explosion

Propositions

Proliferation of polls

New technologies

taking advantage of new rules changes that put the contemporary primary and caucus process in place.[15]

This transformation of the nomination process was only the most visible step in a move away from party-centered elections toward candidate-centered elections.[16] Soon political scientists noticed that a significant incumbency advantage had developed in elections for the House of Representatives: incumbents could win comfortable victories by emphasizing their personal characteristics, constituency service, and individual records even in areas

---

[15] Theodore White, *The Making of the President 1972* (New York: Bantam, 1973), especially Chapter 2.
[16] Martin Wattenberg, *The Decline of American Political Parties, 1952–1996* (Cambridge, MA: Harvard University Press, 1998).

seemingly more hospitable to the opposing party.[17] For their part voters seemed to be putting less weight on their party affiliations, and party cohesion in government broke down as individual office-holders sought to win the support of an increasingly volatile electorate.[18]

Government in the sunshine gained in popularity. Legislatures, boards, and councils around the country opened up their proceedings, allowing citizens to attend and to speak to a greater extent than previously considered advisable in a representative democracy. These same government bodies opened their heretofore closed deliberative proceedings to the public as well. And, increasingly, the actions of elected officials entered into the public record, as legislatures abandoned voice, standing, and other forms of anonymous voting in favor of recorded votes.

Both the courts themselves and Congress liberalized rules of standing so that citizens could use the courts to a much greater extent than previously.[19] A nature lover who had not suffered personal material damage from a new dam could not sue on behalf of salmon in 1960. Today such a right is taken for granted.[20] In associated developments courts that at one time had largely deferred to administrative rule-makers began to take an increasingly active and aggressive role in overseeing the administrative process.[21] Congress even subsidized intervenors in bureaucratic proceedings

---

[17] Gary Jacobson, *The Politics of Congressional Elections* (New York: Longman, 2001): 125–32.
[18] For a recent survey of these developments see Morris Fiorina, "Parties and Partisanship: A 40-Year Retrospective," *Political Behavior* 24 (2002): 93–115.
[19] Richard Stewart, "The Reformation of American Administrative Law." *Harvard Law Review* 88 (1975): 1169–1813.
[20] As a member of Trout Unlimited I certainly regard this as an advance in social welfare.
[21] R. Shep Melnick, *Regulation and the Courts* (Washington, DC: Brookings, 1983).

and allowed them to collect legal fees for challenging agency actions in the courts.

At the local level "maximum feasible participation" became the watchword of the time as the federal government used its sticks and carrots to open up local politics to new groups and subsidized the formation of such groups. And as we noted earlier, there was a huge increase in local government jurisdictions of various types.[22]

Meanwhile an advocacy explosion occurred as thousands of new groups organized and engaged in political activity.[23] Sometimes they circumvented uncooperative legislatures by sponsoring propositions—the use of propositions surged between 1960 and 2000.[24] Politicians became increasingly aware of popular reaction to their actions as polling became a pervasive feature of contemporary society, and new technologies that at first enabled politicians to better advertise to constituents soon got turned around as citizens' groups realized they could use the same technologies to pressure politicians.

In short, these changes and others stripped away the insulation that had long surrounded political institutions and processes, leaving them more exposed to popular scrutiny and far more open to popular participation. Seemingly American democracy became more democratic. Or did it?

---

[22] According to the U.S. Census Bureau, there are now about 86,000 governmental jurisdictions in the United States, most of them at the local level.

[23] Kay Schlozman and John Tierney, *Organized Interests and American Democracy* (New York: Harper and Row, 1986); Jack Walker, *Mobilizing Interest Groups in America* (Ann Arbor, MI: University of Michigan Press,1991); Jonathan Rauch, *Government's End: Why Washington Stopped Working* (New York: Public Affairs, 1999).

[24] A trend decried by some of our leading political commentators. See David Broder, *Democracy Derailed: Initiative Campaigns and the Power of Money* (New York: Harcourt Brace, 2000).

THE HIJACKING OF AMERICAN DEMOCRACY

The three developments just discussed (along with others I have no doubt overlooked) have cumulated and interacted to produce the present disturbing state of American politics. How they have is not immediately obvious. For although government bodies make laws and issue regulations applying to a vastly larger range of economic and social activities, there are also vastly increased opportunities for Americans to participate in making those laws and applying those regulations. The problem is that relatively few people take advantage of those opportunities. Mostly, the purists do.

For most Americans, attending lengthy meetings of city councils, school boards, or planning commissions is not something high on the list of favorite ways to spend an evening. Relaxing after a hard and stressful day's work, spending a little time with the kids, or enjoying a few hours of recreation generally come first. Similarly, when it comes to ways to spend a Saturday afternoon, attending a caucus comes in well below almost anything other than a dentist appointment. Whatever the literal meaning of the Greek, Aristotle is best translated as "Man is by nature a social animal," because the more common alternative "Man is by nature a political animal" is clearly wrong. Most people do not take inherent pleasure in political activity. For most of us, it is costly in time, energy, and resources that we would prefer to devote to other activities. Almost half of us do not even bother to vote in presidential elections. As the young Robert Putnam wrote,

Most men are not political animals. The world of public affairs is not their world. It is alien to them—possibly benevolent, more probably threatening, but nearly always alien. Most men are not interested in politics. Most do not participate in politics.[25]

Who does participate? Who takes advantage of the multitudinous new opportunities to attend evening meetings, write checks, and work in campaigns? While there are a variety of reasons people participate, ranging from the social to the material, probably the most general is that the people who participate are for the most part those who care intensely about some issue or some complex of issues. They have deep policy, programmatic, or ideological commitments. That seems completely obvious—people who care expend their time, energy, and other resources to participate. People who do not care do not make the effort. One does not need a Ph.D. to point that out.

The problem is that people who care deeply also tend to have extreme views on the issues they care deeply about. The first observations to this effect were made by political scientists three-quarters of a century ago, and no doubt politicians have understood the association between intensity and extremity since the first chieftains heard the angry rumblings around the campfires eons ago.[26] Intensity and extremity go together as illustrated by the pairings of common political descriptors. We regularly read and hear about raging liberals but not raging moderates, rabid

---

[25] Robert Putnam, *The Beliefs of Politicians* (New Haven, CT: Yale University Press, 1973): 1.

[26] Floyd Allport and D. A. Hartman. "The Measurement and Motivation of Atypical Opinion in a Certain Group," *American Political Science Review* 19 (1925): 735–60. See also Hadley Cantril, "The Intensity of an Attitude," *Journal of Abnormal and Social Psychology* 41 (1946): 129–35.

conservatives but not rabid middle-of-the-roaders, wishy-washy moderates but not wishy-washy liberals or conservatives, bitter partisans but not bitter independents.[27] To have an intensely held position generally is to hold an extreme position, and vice versa.

Thus, not only is the desire to participate not very widely distributed in the general population, there is a strong bias in how it is distributed. The extremes are overrepresented in the political arena and the center underrepresented. The standard example is the party activists who dominate the presidential selection process. Activists are small minorities even within their own parties—the highest recorded turnout in the Iowa caucuses was 12 percent of the voting age population in 1988 when both parties had competitive nomination contests. Generally the turnout percentage is in single digits. In January of 2004, with no contest on the Republican side, some 120,000 of the most committed Democrats turned out to vote in the Iowa caucuses, about one-sixth as many as the 700,000 Iowans who voted for Al Gore in 2000. The situation is similar in the issue battles waged by the various cause groups. As we discussed in Chapter 4 the terms of the abortion debate are set by the 10 percent or so of the population that occupy each tail of the distribution of abortion attitudes, while the three-quarters of the population of "pro-choice buts" goes largely unheard. Extremists march, work in campaigns, give money, and otherwise push their views more strongly than do moderates.

I emphasize that this pattern of biased participation is broad and pervasive. It extends well beyond partisanship and a few

---

[27] In a column about the Middle East Thomas Friedman wishes for more "fanatical moderates," calling attention to the fact that such people are rare: "Wanted: Fanatical Moderates," *New York Times Op-ed*, November 16, 2003: 13.

prominent issues like abortion, and it extends well below the national level as well. Indeed, the bias may be worst on the local level. Consider the following recent illustration from San Francisco.[28] Residents began complaining that someone was using axes and chain saws to girdle mature trees (eucalyptus, Monterey Pines, and cypress) on city property. Anti-environmentalists? Anti-social vandals? On investigation it turned out that it was citizen tax dollars at work. The city Recreation and Park Department contains a unit called the Natural Areas Program (NAP), which has both paid staff and volunteers. The trees were a casualty of a NAP master plan that among other things called for the eradication of "alien species." On further investigation it turned out that NAP volunteers had already begun restoring poison oak (a native species) to some city parks, and that future plans included replacing the turtles at a city lake with a more genetically correct species of tortoise.

San Francisco is an extremely liberal city and its residents yield to no one in their greenness, but even in San Francisco there is no majority in favor of poison oak. Having been made aware of what one of its tiny specialized agencies was up to, the Park Department appointed an advisory panel to oversee the NAP, "but then it was discovered that most of the organizations on the list [of advisory panel members] consisted of similar native plant supporters."[29] City supervisors then reconstituted the panel to include park users and elected officials.

---

28 This vignette is drawn from Ken Garcia, "S.F. Residents Battling Plant Lovers—Little-Known Group Chopping Down Trees," *San Francisco Chronicle* April 23, 2002: A-13, and "Poison Oak Activists Restrained," *San Francisco Chronicle*, October 1, 2002: A-13.
29 "Poison Oak Activists Restrained": A-13.

While this may seem like an extreme example, lesser examples at the local level are legion. A local official working in concert with a small constituency of committed issue activists formulates a proposal or plan that is far out of the mainstream of community sentiment (environmental and land use restrictions probably are the most common, but sex education in the schools provides some wild examples). At some point the proposal makes it onto the radar screens of normal people who do not participate in obscure government proceedings, a dust-up occurs, and the proposal is rejected or the program revised or terminated amidst acrimonious debate and popular disbelief.

In addition to pushing unrepresentative views on specific issues, two other characteristics of purists are worthy of note. The first is that the issues that motivate them often are different from those that are of most concern to the great mass of ordinary citizens. Most citizens want a secure country, a healthy economy, safe neighborhoods, good schools, affordable health care, and good roads, parks, and other infrastructure. Such issues do get discussed, of course, but a disproportionate amount of attention goes to issues like abortion, gun control, the pledge of allegiance, medical marijuana, and other narrow issues that simply do not motivate the great bulk of the American people. For example, despite the attention it receives in the political arena, abortion does not show up on lists of what citizens say are the most important issues facing the country.[30]

---

[30] Eight polls by five different polling organizations in 2002–2003 asked a version of the "most important problems facing the country" item. None received enough abortion responses to report them as a separate category. http://www.pollingreport.com/ prioriti.htm, accessed January 5, 2004.

Gun control is a particularly illustrative issue.[31] A large majority of the country favors "common sense" gun control provisions—background checks, trigger locks, higher minimum age requirements, registration, prohibitions of high-capacity clips, and so on. But most Americans do not believe that additional restrictions will do much good. Perhaps for that reason few people feel very intensely about gun control—one national poll in the aftermath of Columbine had gun control twelfth in importance on a list of voting issues. Antigun and pro-gun activists are another story, of course, and they fight tooth and nail over what most Americans view as a relatively minor issue. Al Gore staked out a strong position on the issue in 2000, apparently to appeal to gun control activists in the Democratic primaries.[32] A more moderate position on gun control probably would not have cost him any blue states, but it might have kept enough hunters in the Democratic fold (or out of the electorate) to swing 2 percent of the vote in Ohio or Missouri or Tennessee, or 1 percent in New Hampshire. Had Gore carried even one of these states, he would now be president—Florida would have been irrelevant.

Finally, because purists hold their views more intensely than ordinary people do, their operating style differs from that of most people. They are completely certain of their views: they are right and their opponents are wrong. Moreover, their opponents are not just misguided or misinformed, but corrupt, stupid, evil, or all three. There can be no compromise because truth does not

---

[31] The discussion in this paragraph draws on Morris Fiorina and Paul Peterson, *The New American Democracy*, 3rd ed. (New York: Longman, 2003): 150–152.
[32] In addition, Gore's strong antigun position may have been part of his attempt to appeal to women voters on child safety issues.

compromise with error. Their issues are too serious to permit any levity to enter the discussion. Angry attacks substitute for reasoned discussion.

Most adult Americans spend their daily lives working in organizations where courtesy and civility are basic presumptions of how people should deal with each other. Moreover, discussion and negotiation underlie normal decision-making processes in the organizations and institutions of civil society and the economy. Americans contrast the environments in which they live their lives with a political order dominated by activists and elected officials who behave like squabbling children in a crowded sandbox. This is another reason why Americans dislike politics: they are put off by the people who specialize in politics.[33]

In sum, there is a disconnect between the world of contemporary Americans and the political order that purports to represent them. Citizens see a political order that characteristically debates policy proposals more extreme than necessary to address societal issues and community problems, a political order that spends inordinate amounts of time debating policy issues that most citizens do not view as among the more important issues facing the country, and a political order dominated by a political class whose behavior and operating style would be unacceptable outside of politics. Citizens hardly can be blamed if they increasingly regard government as something that tries to do things *to* them rather than *for* them.

---

[33] An Arizona state representative told me that he would look around the ballroom at his election night parties and think "these are the only parties these people ever get invited to."

THREE IMPORTANT CAVEATS

By this point some readers may suspect that my vision of American politics is some kind of utopia akin to *Mr. Rogers' Neighborhood*, where all of us are friends. Far from it; I do not think that in the absence of purist domination of democratic political processes we would all spend our days sitting around singing "Kumbaya." Conflict is the human condition, and conflict is the basis of politics—conflict of wants, conflict of interests, and conflict of values. As Madison wrote in Federalist 51, "But what is government itself but the greatest of all reflections on human nature? If men were angels, no government would be necessary." Government is a necessary evil. Evil because it is inherently coercive and its operations restrict the liberty of some citizens.[34] Necessary, because in its absence even greater evils would occur as a result of some exercising their unrestricted liberty.

All I mean to argue in the preceding pages is that the political order that now exists in the United States creates unnecessary conflicts and indulges itself in conflicts that are the concern of relatively small numbers of unrepresentative people. Often this comes at the expense of attention to conflicts that concern larger numbers of people and leads to inattention to policy solutions that would be widely viewed as progressive.[35]

---

[34] As George Washington put it, "Government is not reason, it is not eloquence—it is force."

[35] A number of recent books propose bold policy proposals to meet important problems in the area of health care, education, and Social Security, as well as point out that political stalemate keeps such proposals off the agenda. My aim in this book has been to explain why the political order is unable and even unwilling to address problems that concern millions of ordinary Americans in a pragmatic nonideological manner. See for example, Michael Lind and Ted Halsted, *The Radical Center: The Future of American Politics* (New York: Anchor, 2002); Matthew Miller, *The Two Percent Solution* (New York: PublicAffairs, 2003). For a forerunner, see E. J. Dionne Jr., *Why Americans Hate Politics* (New York: Simon & Schuster, 1991).

A second, even more important, caveat is that the changes in American politics outlined in the preceding pages are by no means all bad. Few would argue that the United States was better off as a society before the mid-1960s expansion in the scope of government. The great progress toward ending racial discrimination alone falsifies any such claim. Similarly, the treatment of women, the handicapped, the aged, and other vulnerable categories indisputably has improved society. So has the treatment of our environment and our natural resources. Like my colleagues who are economists, I believe that in many cases there were more efficient and less coercive ways to achieve many of these laudable goals, but if the choice is between what government did and its having done nothing, the answer seems clear to me. My argument is simply that when combined with the participatory turn, the expansion in the scope of government allowed various kinds of fanatics to exert an undue degree of control over the political agenda.

A final caveat should go without saying, but I have learned from various talks that it does not. Nothing in these pages advocates the suppression of minority points of view. Sometimes extremists are right and a majority eventually adopts their once-extreme views. The abolitionists held views that most at the time considered extreme, and certainly the intensity with which some of them held their views was demonstrated in arenas like Bloody Kansas and events like John Brown's raid. Intense minorities have every right to freedom of speech and association, and when peaceful advocacy proves futile, they can engage in civil disobedience. When they do, they should expect to be sanctioned by the societal majority: over time their sacrifices may convince society of their views. That said, there is no reason to support a political order that disproportionately enhances the power of intense minorities.

CAN ANYTHING BE DONE?

"Clowns to left of me, jokers to the right, here I am, stuck in the middle with you."
(from Stealer's Wheel, *Stuck in the Middle With You*)

The chorus of this 1973 pop hit could well serve as the anthem of the American people. How might we diminish the influence of the clowns and jokers and expand the influence of the middle? I am not optimistic. There will be no help from the political class itself. The activists who gave rise to the notion of a culture war, in particular, and a deeply polarized politics, in general, for the most part are sincere. *They* are polarized. Leaders of conservative Christian groups allied with the Republican Party sincerely believe they are fighting a culture war, as do leaders and activists in pro-choice and gay rights groups allied with the Democratic Party. That they are small, unrepresentative minorities does not alter the fact that these and numerous other interest group activists feel strongly about their issues and will vote, work, and contribute in support of them.

Nor will most politicians be of much help. Like interest group leaders, many candidates and office-holders sincerely believe they are engaged in a war. Some are themselves purists who were activists before winning office. Others see instrumental reasons for acting like purists. Each party has a base composed of people particularly sensitive to certain issues. Increasingly, professional campaigners seem to believe that mobilizing the base is the most important component of a winning electoral strategy, a belief that may be a self-fulfilling prophecy if appeals to the base result in moderate voters turning off and tuning out. So, however misplaced from the standpoint of the welfare of the larger country, an emphasis on cultural and other conflicts not of particular interest to the majority appears to be an integral part of contemporary electoral politics.

The media potentially could be of some use. When an activist spokesperson makes a pronouncement, a critical media could ask "Whom do you speak for?" "How many citizens do you speak for?" "When did they appoint you as their spokesperson?" The media could even cease its unconsidered use of the neutral term "activist" and use terms that are often more accurate—exhibition- ist, crackpot, blowhard. None of this will come to pass however, for despite pious pronouncements about the role of the media as the guardian of democracy, the media consist largely of profit- sector enterprises that will continue to behave as such. That means an emphasis on differences among Americans rather than com- monalities. The commercial success of the newspapers and news shows depends on good story lines, and conflict is a good story line. "Americans agree on core values" is not a headline that edi- tors expect to sell newspapers. "Citizens describe themselves as moderates" is not a good lead for the evening news. A red and blue battleground over which the Democrats and Republicans wage war is a news frame that fits the selection principles of the news industry.

Political scientists are notoriously loath to suggest reforms. As a profession we tend to be conservative with a small "c." One reason is that more than most people we realize how little we truly know about the operation of political processes and institutions, and, consequently, how likely it is that proposed reforms will prove ineffectual or even counterproductive. The long, frustrating history of campaign finance reform is a good example, but arguably, almost all reforms have had some unforeseen negative consequence. Nevertheless, I offer three possibilities that would likely improve our politics, although I stress that these are not magic bullets, either alone or in combination. Moreover, although they would probably increase the representativeness of electoral politics at the state and national levels, they would do little to redress the unrepresentative nature of local politics that requires time-consuming participation in the deliberations of councils and boards. The latter seems to me to be a far more difficult problem.

PRIMARY REFORM

In Chapter 7 we discussed how the abstract median voter model provides the logic underlying the traditional observation that two-party competition has centrist tendencies.[36] In the real world, however, that abstract logic can be overridden by factors not in the model. One of these factors is primary elections that select the candidates who will stand in the general election.

In 1994 California Republican Governor Pete Wilson won reelection in a landslide, Republican candidates won four of the six other statewide races for state office, and Republicans defeated

---

[36] When there is more than one issue dimension there is generally no equilibrium, but a variety of alternative solution notions nevertheless continues to support the conclusion of centrist tendencies in two-party competition.

four Democratic House incumbents. Seemingly, Bill Clinton's 1992 victory in the state had been only a hiccup in a long Republican era that began with the election of Ronald Reagan as governor in 1966. That appearance was wrong. In 1996 Clinton hammered Republican Robert Dole, and four years later Al Gore easily bested George W. Bush. The hapless condition of the California Republican Party became strikingly clear in 2002 when they could not defeat Gray Davis, a personally unpopular Democratic governor who had mishandled a state energy crisis and allowed a historic budget crisis to develop. In fact, Democrats won all the statewide races in 2002 for the first time in California history. In less than a decade California had changed its hue from dark red to dark blue.

What happened? The California Republican Party was captured by its extreme social conservative elements, and its electoral fortunes promptly plummeted.[37] Many analyses identify Senator Barbara Boxer as one of the most liberal members of the U.S. Senate, seemingly a candidate vulnerable to defeat at the hands of a Republican moderate, but she is a two-time winner. Similarly, the unasked question in the 2003 recall of Democratic Governor Davis was how such a personally unpopular governor, saddled with energy and budget crises, could have been reelected in the first place? The answer both to Senator Boxer's survival and to Davis's reelection lies in the old political saw that "you can't beat

---

[37] Although the reversal of Republican and Democratic fortunes in California often is attributed to the growth in the proportion of minority, especially Latino, voters, preliminary analysis indicates that the areas of greatest Republican loss were economically upscale areas that registered relatively high levels of support for environmental and gun control initiatives, and relatively low levels of support for antiabortion and antigay initiatives. Josh Benson, "From Reagan Country to Clinton Capital: The Political Transformation of California," Senior Thesis, Stanford University Political Science Department, 2003.

somebody with nobody." In primary elections California Republicans nominate hard-core conservatives whose appeal is too limited to defeat even flawed Democratic candidates.[38]

In 1996 almost 60 percent of California voters, including majorities of both registered Republicans and Democrats, approved Proposition 198, a ballot initiative sponsored by Tom Campbell, the kind of Republican social moderate who has trouble winning California primaries.[39] The proposition called for a "blanket primary," an unusual system in which all voters—Democrats, Republicans, minor party adherents, and the non-aligned—can work their way down the same ballot, voting for a Democratic candidate for one office, a Republican candidate for another, a Libertarian candidate for yet another, and so on, with the leading vote getter in each party for each office advancing to the general election. The intent was to increase turnout and to dilute the extreme voices who dominate closed primaries by allowing moderate candidates to win by attracting the support of (an increased number of) independents and moderate members of the opposing party. Called the "blanket" primary by its supporters, critics derided it as a "free love" primary (because voters did not have to make any commitment to a party). Both major

---

[38] Boxer was initially elected in 1992, running against Bruce Herschensohn, a far-right Los Angeles radio and TV commentator. In 1998 she handily defeated a Republican who flip-flopped on abortion and gay rights as he was caught between the conservative party base and the larger more moderate electorate. Her luck appears to be holding in 2004. In 2002 Davis was narrowly reelected running against Bill Simon, a conservative businessman with little political experience. Interestingly, less than a year after reelecting Davis, a larger number of Californians than had voted in 2002 turned out to recall him, and a larger number than had voted for Davis in 2002 voted to replace him with Arnold Schwarzenegger, a political novice. In the exception that proves the rule, Schwarzenegger is the kind of socially moderate Republican who can win elections in California. The unusual nature of the recall election saved the California Republican Party from itself.

[39] Campbell had lost to Herschensohn for the honor of opposing Boxer in 1992. Many analysts thought he would have defeated Boxer had he gotten through the primary.

parties as well as various minor parties immediately filed suit to overturn the blanket primary as an unconstitutional infringement on their rights of free association, such unified opposition by the parties confirming voters' beliefs that the blanket primary was a good idea.[40]

The challenge wended its way through the courts until in 2000 the U.S. Supreme Court by a 7-2 margin held for the parties and threw out the blanket primary.[41] My sympathies lie with the two dissenters (Justice Stevens joined by Justice Ginsburg), who did not understand why the associational rights of political parties should outweigh the right of voters to structure the electoral process—the very basis of democratic government, *whose operation they pay for*—however they please. But Justice Scalia, who wrote for the majority, explicitly noted the constitutionality of other primary formats, such as Louisiana's nonpartisan run-off primary.[42] In this primary, all the candidates for the same office are listed together. If one candidate wins a majority of the vote on the first round, he or she is elected. If not, the top two finishers wage a second, run-off campaign to determine the winner. At the time of this writing supporters are working to qualify such a ballot initiative in California.

The run-off primary should have somewhat the same consequences as the blanket primary. Given more choices one would

---

[40] "Part of its appeal may have been its antagonists. State GOP Chairman John Herrington bemoaned the appeal to 'the mindless middle,' " Ronald D. Elving, "Californians Explore 'Jungle Primaries.'" 1996. *Pundits & Prose*. CNN-All Politics. http://www.cnn.com/allpolitics/1996/analysis/pundits .prose/elving/elving1.shtml, accessed November 19, 2003. For wide-ranging discussions of California's experience with the blanket primary see Bruce Cain and Elisabeth Gerber, eds., *Voting at the Political Fault Line* (Berkeley, CA: University of California Press, 2002).
[41] *California Democratic Party et al v. Jones*.
[42] Ibid., 18.

expect more voters to participate, and moderate Republicans or Democrats might defeat hard-core partisans with the support of independents and moderate voters from the other party. That possibility troubles hard-core partisans of both parties, of course. The worst outcome is to lose an office, but a close second is to win it with a candidate of your own party insufficiently committed to your principles; some hard-core partisans even rank the second outcome lower than the first.

The problem with nonpartisan run-off primaries inheres in one of their many nicknames. Sometimes called "jungle primaries," they allow the distinct possibility that fringe candidates can make the runoff, as when David Duke, a former member of the Ku Klux Klan, made the runoff for governor of Louisiana in 1991. It is highly unlikely, although not impossible, that such candidates can win a major party nomination in a primary, but with several Republicans, several Democrats, and various other candidates on the ballot, the top two finishers might have relatively small proportions of the total vote and neither may have very widespread appeal. Still, high thresholds (signatures, filing fees) for making the ballot can reduce the number of fringe candidates, and the desire of voters not to waste their votes on long shots or no shots should work in favor of candidates with broad appeal.

REDISTRICTING REFORM

As we noted in Chapter 2, recent national elections have been exceedingly close—*in the aggregate*. This is most apparent in elections for the House of Representatives since 1996, where the parties have split the aggregate vote nearly evenly and control of the

House has been at stake in each election. But despite the close division of the aggregate vote as well as the close division of seats, when we look a little closer at the statistics, an interesting feature of congressional elections emerges: as elections have gotten closer in the aggregate, the number of competitive elections has declined. In 2000, when the presidential race was a cliff-hanger, only seventy-four of the 435 House seats were won by margins of less than 55 percent. In 2002, following the decennial reapportionment and redistricting cycle, the number of such competitive districts fell to forty-seven.

The number of competitive congressional districts declined in the mid-1960s and stayed low through most of the 1970s and 1980s. Although redistricting was suspected as a cause of that earlier decline, academic research found little support for that suspicion.[43] Competition increased in the 1990s but then fell in 2000 and fell again in 2002. Most observers believe that the redistricting that occurred in 2001–2002 had a good bit to do with the latter decline in competitive seats—the parties behaved conservatively, concentrating on protecting their seats rather than attempting to capture those of the opposition.[44] The result was a bipartisan gerrymander that left almost 90 percent of U.S. House seats safely in the hands of one or the other of the two parties, despite the close division of the aggregate vote.

To appreciate the effect of alternative districting arrangements, consider the simplified example illustrated in Figures 8.1A

---

[43] John Ferejohn, "On the Decline in Competition in Congressional Elections," *American Political Science Review* 71 (1977): 166–76. For a more recent and more conditional analysis cf. Gary Cox and Jonathan Katz, *Elbridge Gerry's Salamander* (Cambridge, England: Cambridge University Press, 2002).
[44] Gregory Gilroux, "Remap's Clear Trend: Incumbent Protection," *CQ Weekly*, November 3, 2001: 2627–32.

and 8.1B. A hypothetical state consists of 40 percent Democrats, 40 percent Republicans, and 20 percent Independents. The state is rectangular in shape and people are evenly distributed over its

FIGURE 8.1A
Bipartisan Gerrymander to Maximize Safe Seats

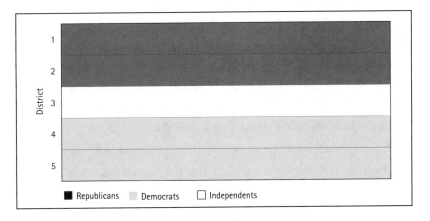

FIGURE 8.1B
Redistricting to Maximize Competitive Seats

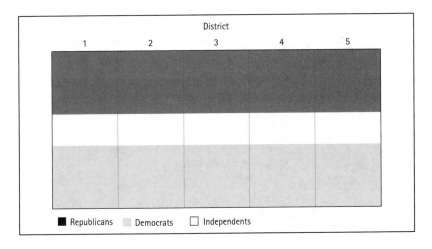

area, but partisans are concentrated: the Democrats all live in the northern two-fifths of the state, Republicans in the southern two-fifths, Independents in the middle fifth. Assume the citizens elect a five-member legislature from single-member districts of equal population. Among the many possibilities, one would be to draw five districts horizontally, as in Figure 8.1A. This districting arrangement results in two safe Democratic districts in the north, two safe Republican districts in the south, and one competitive district in the middle.

Alternatively, one could draw district lines vertically, as in Figure 8.1B. This districting arrangement would result in five competitive districts, each containing equal numbers of Democrats and Republicans, with Independents holding the balance.

Politics under the alternative districting arrangements probably would be much different. Under the horizontal arrangement, the safe Democrats and Republicans only fear a primary challenge, since the other party has no support in their areas. In the middle district a moderate Democrat or Republican would be elected by independent voters. Whichever party she came from she would be under fierce pressure from her fellow partisans from safe districts to follow a strictly partisan line in the legislature.

Under the second districting arrangement, all the districts would be competitive. A party could win anywhere from none to five seats in an election, but no one could win with the support of only their partisans. Independents hold the balance in all districts, providing a strong incentive for the candidates to appeal to the middle.

Generalizing from this stylized example, the present nasty situation in Congress and some state legislatures, such as California's, results in part from districting arrangements akin to that depicted in Figure 8.1A. Most incumbents have little to fear in the general election, so they concentrate on heading off challenges from their party extremes. If we could move somewhat more toward the arrangement in Figure 8.1B, a more moderate politics should result. The problem is that the party representatives in the state legislatures draw the lines in most cases, and for a variety of reasons, they do not want competitive districts.

Since the important one-person, one-vote decisions handed down by the U.S. Supreme Court in the mid-1960s, the court has intervened actively in the legislative redistricting process but so far has limited its conception of equal representation. The courts closely examine population equality, demanding a degree of inter-district equality that is truly preposterous.[45] And the courts have willingly taken up challenges involving questions of racial fairness. Until very recently, however, the courts have hesitated to consider the question of partisan or bipartisan gerrymandering.[46] In *Vieth v. Judelirer,* decided in April 2004, a 5–4 majority of the U.S. Supreme Court declined to invalidate a Pennsylvania redistricting plan on the grounds that it was an unconstitutional partisan gerrymander. The court left open (barely) the possibility of considering future cases, however, so the courts may extend their reach in the coming years.

---

[45] For example, in a 2002 Pennsylvania decision, a three-judge panel of the Federal Appeals Court threw out a redistricting plan because the most and least populous districts differed by nineteen residents. Because of errors, deaths, births, and moves, census data are not accurate to within nineteen residents in a congressional district (approximately 650,000 people) by the time they are recorded, let alone by the time the first election in the new districts occurs. Jonathan Allen, "Court Puts Pa. Primaries in Doubt," *CQ Weekly,* April 13, 2002: 963.

[46] In a partisan gerrymander, one party attempts to screw the other. In a bipartisan gerrymander both parties agree on a plan to divvy up the seats.

In sum, one avenue toward moderating American politics would be to remove redistricting from the purview of legislatures and place it in the hands of (preferably nonpartisan) appointed commissions. But rather than have the legislature approve the final plan, skip the legislature and submit it to popular referendum. Obviously, the likelihood of adoption of such a reform by a state legislature is minimal. Popular referendum probably would be the only way to adopt it.

INCREASING PARTICIPATION

If political participation is correlated with greater intensity and extremity of views, then other things being equal, any increase in participation entails an increase in participation by less intense and less extreme people. Thus, reforms that increase participation have the potential to lower the decibel level of American politics and increase its attentiveness to mainstream concerns. The obvious targets are reform of registration and voting procedures that would make both easier. Political scientists have given this subject a good deal of attention and the most detailed research suggests that maximum easing of registration and voting procedures would increase turnout in presidential elections by eight to fifteen percentage points.[47]

In his 1997 presidential address to the American Political Science Association, Arend Lijphart called for compulsory voting, an idea utterly foreign to Americans but widely accepted in other

---

[47] Ruy Teixeira, *The Disappearing American Voter* (Washington, DC: Brookings, 1992): ch. 4.

world democracies.[48] Unfavorable comparisons of voting turnout in the United States with turnout elsewhere generally omit any mention that 90+ percent turnout figures in other democracies often are produced by compulsory voting laws. Usually these levy fines for failure to vote, although Greece provides for jail terms, a penalty that is never enforced. Italy uses a mixture of carrots and sticks, subsidizing travel back to one's place of registration, but stamping nonvoters' papers with "did not vote" and posting their names on community bulletin boards. Judging by the outraged reaction of my students, the principal objection to such laws is that people should not be forced to vote when they may not like any of the candidates. This objection could be easily met— permitting submission of a blank ballot, or putting a "none of the above" option on the ballot, for example.

There is a vein of political science research that discounts the political effect of increased turnout. Analysts make the counterfactual assumption that everyone votes, and then compare the distributions of political attitudes and candidate preferences between the hypothetical expanded electorate with those in the actual electorate. Such analyses typically report only small differences.[49] Without plunging deeply into a discussion of false consciousness, the problem with such analyses lies in the assumption that "other things remain the same." If the presidential electorate were to nearly double, and the off-year electorate to nearly triple, it is likely that parties and candidates would make different appeals to capture the support of the new voters who would now be showing

---

[48] "Unequal Participation: Democracy's Unresolved Dilemma," *American Political Science Review* 91 (1997): 1–14.
[49] Teixeira, *Disappearing American Voter*: 86–101 reports his own results and summarizes others.

up at the polls. There is no reason to believe that their preferences would be the same as when they are not in the electorate. In particular, if it were known that a huge influx of politically unattached, relatively moderate people were going to vote, the incentive for candidates to move toward the center would increase.

While I sympathize with Professor Lijphart's argument for compulsory voting, the major problem with advocating it seems to me a practical one. Americans are called on to vote so frequently that it would be unreasonable to require them to vote on any and all occasions when elections were held.[50] Most other democracies vote far less often for far fewer offices than Americans do. The only way compulsory voting would be feasible in the United States would be to "combine up" elections, as was the case roughly between the 1870s and the 1940s. Elect presidents, governors, U.S. Representatives, and state and local officials, as well as vote on propositions, bond issues, and so forth on the same day. Even so, with primaries added in, and shorter terms of office than elsewhere, compulsory voting still would ask a lot of the electorate.

A FINAL THOUGHT

My hope is that my present inability to think of more persuasive ways to improve American politics reflects my inability to think outside the box of traditional forms of participation. These involve physical presence in most cases, and that is too high a price to pay for many or most contemporary Americans, especially

---

[50] Anthony King, Running Scared: *Why America's Politicians Campaign Too Much and Govern Too Little* (New York: Free Press, 1996).

at the local level.[51] But we are in the midst of a revolution in communications technology that might open up entirely new avenues of political participation. Much nonsense has been written about electronic town halls, instantaneous referenda voting, and so forth, but we should not throw out the baby with the bathwater. It may be that the often-decried ability of splinter groups to locate each other over the Internet is more than offset by the far greater ease of mass participation that the Internet allows. To note the most obvious possibility, at some future date, when Internet connections are as ubiquitous as telephones, it might be possible to require that before taking effect every board or council decision must receive the electronic votes of a majority of a given percentage of the citizenry in its jurisdiction.[52] Any such proposal would need thorough public debate, of course, but it illustrates the kinds of new democratic possibilities that may be available to our children.[53]

---

[51] I have the greatest respect for the motives of theoretically minded colleagues who advocate strong forms of deliberative democracy, but as an empirically minded social scientist I think their proposals run counter to everything we know about mass political behavior.

[52] In the New England town where I once lived, concern that low attendance at Town Meeting was producing unrepresentative decisions stimulated some residents to advocate a requirement that any Town Meeting decision should appear on the ballot at the next regularly scheduled town election before taking effect. Betsy Bilodeau, "It's Time to Change Town Meeting," *Concord Journal*, March 5, 1998: 7.

[53] The debate already has begun. See, for example, Jennifer Stromer-Galley, "Voting and the Public Sphere: Conversations on Internet Voting," *PS: Political Science and Politics* 36 (2003): 727–31.

Index